a mennonite

WOMAN

*To Paul, to my parents, and
to Grandma Ruth*

a mennonite WOMAN

Exploring Spiritual Life and Identity

DAWN RUTH NELSON

Foreword by Alan Kreider

Cascadia
Publishing House
Telford, Pennsylvania

Cascadia Publishing House LLC orders, information, reprint permissions:
contact@cascadiapublishinghouse.com
1-215-723-9125
126 Klingerman Road, Telford PA 18969
www.CascadiaPublishingHouse.com

Library of Congress Cataloguing-in-Publication Data
Nelson, Dawn Ruth, 1952-
A Mennonite woman : exploring spiritual life and identity / Dawn Ruth
Nelson ; foreword by Alan Kreider.
  p. cm.
Includes bibliographical references (p.   ).
ISBN-13: 978-1-931038-70-6 (5.5 x 8.5" trade pbk. : alk. paper)
ISBN-10: 1-931038-70-8 (5.5 x 8.5" trade pbk. : alk. paper)
1. Mennonites. 2. Spirituality--Mennonites. 3. Ruth, Susan, 1909-2005.
4. Nelson, Dawn Ruth, 1952- I. Title.

BX8121.3.N46 2010
248.4'897--dc22

2009048120

17 16 15 13 12 11 10   10 9 8 7 6 5 4 3 2 1

CONTENTS

AUTHOR'S PREFACE

Since I finished the major work on my book, many additional and important books on Anabaptist-Mennonite spirituality have appeared. The very number of new books corroborates my thesis: We are experiencing a time of intense searching for spiritual resources in the Mennonite tradition. So even a recent list added at the end of my bibliography will soon be outdated.

However, at the risk of ignoring others, I will mention two of the newer books. *Take Our Moments and Our Days: An Anabaptist Prayerbook,* is a wonderful response to the need for a book of communal prayer enabling Mennonites to immerse ourselves in daily Scripture reading. The *Anabaptist Prayerbook* includes what the authors call "Anabaptist DNA" in the choice of Scriptures and in the focus on a daily call to discipleship. In the second book, C. Arnold Snyder has offered an account of Anabaptist spirituality for the Orbis Books' series, "Traditions of Christian Spirituality." This book, *Following in the Footsteps of Christ: The Anabaptist Tradition,* breaks important new ground and raises questions about how Anabaptism is practiced today.

These newer developments in the ongoing search for depth in our faith and for faithfulness to Christ give me hope. I sense that God is calling us into the future, steeped in the past but faithful to a God who is always moving: "I am about to do a new thing; now it springs forth, do you not perceive it?" (Isa. 43: 19a).

—*Dawn Ruth Nelson*
  Harleysville, Pennsylvania

FOREWORD

"What is Mennonite spirituality?" The Irish Jesuit who talked to Dawn Ruth Nelson in 1983 has not been the only one to ask this question. Others also have wondered: since the Mennonites lack frequent Eucharistic worship and have no explicit tradition of spiritual writing, what forms them to be Christians of peace and justice, simplicity, and community? Or, more disturbingly, what forms Mennonites to be Christians who feel they ought to embody these virtues but know that they don't—and who feel the disparity between profession and reality with what Dawn Ruth Nelson calls "desperation"? What resources can enable contemporary Mennonites in postmodern, post-Christendom Western cultures to live the Christian life as Mennonite theology tells them they ought to live it? In this book, Dawn Ruth Nelson explores these questions with perceptiveness, vulnerability, humor and, above all, hope.

Of this book's special contributions, I will point to three. One is the author's resolute realism. Dawn (I use her first name because I know her well) is a product of late twentieth-century Mennonite idealism. In the late 1970s I was among the Mennonites in England who perceived that the "troubles" in Northern Ireland, in which Protestants and Catholics were engaged in a brutalizing civil war, was a blight on the beautiful "emerald isle" and also a hard-to-refute argument against the Christian gospel. When we issued a call to North American Mennonites to come to Ireland to live the gospel of reconciliation as a peace church, Dawn and her husband Paul were among those who

7

responded. They did so at great personal cost. They worked tirelessly in the peace movement; they learned to survive in one of the roughest areas of Dublin; they lived in intentional community in an overcrowded house; and they had the highest expectations for their own contribution. It was a recipe for burnout, which is what led Dawn to talk to the Irish Jesuit. And to make retreats at abbeys. And to build the significant friendship which she and the other Dublin Mennonites enjoyed with the Cistercian monk Eoin de Bhaldraithe.

"burnout"

Dawn came to see that she could not live the Mennonite vision of discipleship with the spiritual resources she had brought to Ireland, and she found some Catholics who ministered to her "desperate need for a more meaningful prayer life, a deeper spirituality, a closer connection to God." Dawn had discovered what sensitive missionaries always learn—that there is something in the people to whom they are sent that is a source of healing for them.

She also discovered that the Mennonite tradition was contributing significant things to Brother Eoin and other Irish people, both Catholic and Protestant. Mission, Dawn notes in this book, involves an exchange of gifts. And the gift that Dawn received was infinitely precious—an impetus to learn to pray, to pursue her relationship with Jesus so she could follow Jesus more faithfully. This led Dawn, upon her return from Ireland to Pennsylvania in 1991, to study spirituality and Christian formation.

2.

The book's second special contribution, its analysis of narratives, is a result of her studies. Dawn sensed that the Mennonites of earlier generations had known how to pray; at least her grandmother had. So Dawn arranged to talk extensively with Susan Alderfer Ruth (1909-2005) to get her story. How did Susan pray? How did she learn to be a Christian? What did she think was important?

prayer

The chapter that records these conversations is a treasure; and it may well inspire other Mennonites to talk to their parents and grandparents about their spiritual practices. Dawn knew that her grandmother Susan was a remarkable, loving, serving Christian who embodied the best in Anabaptist values. Conservative in garb, Susan was ever experimental in finding ways to learn about the world, to make peace and to serve the weak. Yet Dawn discovered that what enabled her grandmother to live in this inviting way was an embodied but inarticulate spiritual formation rooted in community and place that, in an age of mobility and the Internet, seemed irretrievable. Dawn's comparison of her own narrative, as a cosmopolitan, urban Mennonite, with her grandmother's convinced her that there was no way she could live the Anabaptist values that she so admired in her grandmother unless she became thoughtfully articulate about spirituality and was open to being "chastened and enriched" by other, non-Anabaptist traditions. Dawn could bring her narrative into continuity with her grandmother's, but only if other Christians came to her aid.

3.　　This leads to Dawn's third special contribution: her willingness to propose new approaches that are spiritually perceptive and pastorally constructive. One proposal is that we ponder the story of a group of Mennonites in Portland, Oregon, and then at Associated Mennonite Biblical Seminary who were learning to take spiritual formation seriously. Prophetic figures like Marcus Smucker and Marlene Kropf helped individual Mennonites—and an entire seminary—to pray. It has not been easy; Dawn notes the ongoing struggle of Mennonites to take spirituality as seriously as they take ethics.

Dawn's second proposal, based on her own experience and study, is that Mennonites today develop what she calls "a Mennonite spirituality for the twenty-first century." The six elements of this spirituality are rooted in the Christian gospel and the deep Mennonite tradition, realistic about the contemporary Western culture's impediments to the spiritual life, and practical. Informed by the wider Christian tradition, these elements would all be familiar to Susan Alderfer Ruth. "God in the ordinary," nonconformity, community, service, *Gelassenheit,* the centrality of Jesus—all are classically Anabaptist. It is not accidental that the sixth of Dawn's proposals has to do with Jesus Christ: "to be conformed to Christ, to be formed by Christ, we need to spend very significant time with his words and in his presence, corporately and privately." It sounds like Hans Denck! Dawn's writing helps her readers make this vision their own and live it.

Dawn Ruth Nelson's *A Mennonite Woman* is personal, profound, and practical. Christians who long for the spiritual resources to live the Anabaptist Vision in today's multilayered world will find it immensely useful. And, if it inspires its readers to listen to the spiritual journeys of their grandparents as well as to the wisdom of other traditions, it could lead Christians to find "a Mennonite spirituality" that is a gift to the entire Christian church.

—*Alan Kreider, Elkhart, Indiana, teaches Church History and Mission at Associated Mennonite Biblical Seminary in Elkhart. For twenty-six years a missionary with Mennonite Mission Network in the United Kingdom, he is author, with Eleanor Kreider, of* Worship and Mission After Christendom *(Milton Keynes, UK: Paternoster Press, 2009).*

INTRODUCTION: WHY SPIRITUAL PRACTICES MATTER TO ME AND TO MISSION

The shooting of <u>ten Amish girls on October 2, 2006</u>, and the subsequent media coverage of the internal Amish dynamics of forgiveness and mutual support, engaged the world. There was the good news, on television! There was the gospel—right on the same TV shows where we normally see cycles of violence and bad news. It was a communal example of "turning the other cheek" that was immensely life-affirming and hopeful. It took the spotlight away from evil, away from the horror of the murders, and put it on Jesus Christ's example. Actually, the one Amish man I saw interviewed on TV, with his back to the camera, put the spotlight on his own sin, by asking, "How can we not forgive when Christ has forgiven each of us?"

The tragedy led to soul-searching on the part of many, including the close cousins of the Amish, the Mennonites. In the October 23, 2006, issue of *Mennonite Weekly Review*, Paul Schrag, a Mennonite editor, asked other Mennonites if we could be nonconformed in the way these Amish were and still be part of the real world in a way—he implies—they are not. Mennonites descend from the same sixteenth-century Anabaptist tradition that Amish people do; their spirituality is the same in many

11

ways. This act of forgiveness is a special challenge to Mennonites, who share the Anabaptist theology on which it was based but claim we do not need to be different in outward ways—the ways of dress and travel and houses that are buggy-distance apart—like the Amish. Paul Schrag calls the editorial, "Virtue for the Real World."[1] "Here, in full media glare," he says,

> was Christianity as it is rarely practiced by the masses of Christians who've blended in with the world. People recognized the Amish act of forgiveness as an expression of the Christian faith's highest ideals. But it also seemed otherworldly, befitting those who have separated themselves from the world. Mennonites are euniquely placed to resolve this paradox of irrelevant virtue.

Schrag uses the term "irrelevant"—but ongoing popular fascination with the Amish deaths at Nickel Mines and profound subsequent reflection on the part of the media gives us pause.[2] Schrag goes on to talk about the "different choices about engaging the world" that Amish and Mennonites have made. In fact, it is what caused them to separate three hundred years ago.

The Amish believe faithfulness requires conformity within their group and non-conformity to everyone else. Acculturated Mennonites, on the other hand, permit diversity within the church and a great deal of conformity to the world. Ironically, the opposite approaches may produce similar results. Few want to join the Amish, because they are too different. Perhaps too few want to join mainstream Mennonite churches because we aren't different enough.[3]

Perhaps it is time for new discussions of an old word Schrag uses here: *nonconformity*. "The radical 'differentness' of Amish forgiveness got the world's attention. At the same time, Amish 'otherness' made it hard to see their actions as a model," Schrag says. Is Christian otherness missional? In what ways does our otherness reflect a genuine Christ-life and draw people in? In what ways does it exclude? In what ways are Christians no longer other at all? These are ongoing questions of faith for all Christians. For Schrag, it led to a manifesto for his own denomination:

> [W]hat if Mennonites practiced Amish-like virtue without Amish-like separation? We would relate to the world with both nonconformity and engagement. Our differentness would show not in rules about clothing and transportation but in acts of Christlike love. Our nonconformity would rise from placing loyalty to the kingdom of God above all earthly authorities. Our commitment to peace, easy to dismiss when practiced by a separated people, would present a challenging alternative to the futility of the world's violence.[4]

What if, indeed! The editorial, and the events following the shooting of the Amish girls, brought me back to a thesis I'd written on Mennonite spiritual formation several years earlier.[5] I'd been struggling to rewrite it for non-academic readers. I'd wondered if there was any point.

This editorial fired me up once again—to contribute to a dialogue on these very questions of separation, engagement, nonconformity, and virtue: *What if* some Christians would practice Amish-like virtue without Amish-like separation? Is that possible? Is it possible to be that self-sacrificial without the immense communal support the Amish experienced after the shootings, evidenced by the visiting and mutual care for the farms of the grieving families, or by the funerals?

How have Mennonite and Amish communities for centuries spiritually formed Christians whose natural response when confronted with evil, is Christ-like forgiveness—whose response to world wars was to develop service opportunities instead? What is it about Amish community life—about Amish communal structures and spiritual formation—that made this kind of forgiving response nearly automatic, uniform, and Christ-based? Does their culture of mutual support, more than our culture of individualism, serve them well in a crisis, as does their attitude of yieldedness to God?[6]

Are there in fact many interlocking pieces to this spiritual formation that enable them to be peaceful, forgiving, to emulate Christ because of great strength internally and communally, that we can learn from—whether as modern Mennonites or as Christians who are not Mennonites but simply hope for a better world?

Nine days after the murder of the Amish girls at Nickel Mines, emerging church leader Brian MacLaren spoke at a Mennonite college in Indiana and confirmed the importance of the Anabaptist style of Christianity that produced the amazing forgiveness response of the Amish.[7] As a reporter told it, "Christian author Brian McLaren lauded the Amish for their willingness to forgive their children's assailant. 'I don't think anyone has ever done a better job of sharing the message of the gospel,' McLaren said Oct. 11 at Goshen College. 'The Amish behavior mystified the world.'"[8]

No one "has ever done a better job of sharing the message of the gospel." MacLaren is saying here that this is the best mission he's seen. This is not our usual picture of sharing the gospel. In circles where the word *missional* is key, this statement should cause reflection. The Amish behavior did actually mystify the whole world—from the people reporting on the phenomenon locally to those connected only by Internet—the good news reached around the globe.[9]

"In public lectures Oct. 11-12," according to the report,

> McLaren called on Mennonites and other Anabaptists to share more loudly and broadly the distinctives of peacemaking, community and discipleship. "We so desperately need, as we move into this emerging culture, *to learn to live a life of Christ instead of just going to church.*" McLaren said. "You need to let your knowledge rub off on others" (italics mine).[10]

Mennonites need to share their desire to live a life of Christ—what they have called "discipleship"—with others in this emerging culture, to be missional.

These recent events took me back to the subject I'd been wrestling with for twenty years, and back to the thesis I'd written on Mennonite spirituality. It all began with the question, "What is Mennonite spirituality?" that a priest who was an Irish Jesuit, Michael Paul Gallagher, asked me in 1987 when I went to him for spiritual direction. We were sitting in his room at the Manresa retreat center beside Dublin Bay. I was then living on the north side of Dublin as a Mennonite peace worker; I had been there eight years, experiencing life on the mission frontlines, and had asked to be trained in this Jesuit program for spiritual directors.

His question was one I couldn't answer. I had never thought about it before. Mennonite spirituality was a way of life, it had seemed to me, not something theoretical you could describe in words or concepts. I had been living it; I could hardly see it clearly enough to describe. It was too close.

But he was trying to understand my spirituality and had never met a Mennonite before—good spiritual directors never try to move a person out of their own spiritual framework. And it was an important question—one that stuck with me for many years. I kept thinking about it.

The next time I went back to Michael Paul Gallagher's Manresa center again for an overnight silent retreat, I remember contrasting my experience of this Catholic center with my usual experiences at Mennonite retreat centers. In the morning at breakfast at Manresa, cold cereal was the only option, and to me the coldness just felt magnified by the other participants in the retreat, who were all silent, not talking, as we puttered around putting cereal and milk in our bowls. I longed for a Mennonite place like Spruce Lake retreat center and the hot breakfasts and warm talk and even perhaps the singing of "I Owe the Lord a Morning Song." Was that Mennonite spirituality? Good food, lots of talking in community, and four-part singing?

It's interesting to me to note that I first reached out for spiritual direction at a time of great personal need—when the other American missionary couple we worked with went on furlough for a year and I was the defacto leader of the Dublin Mennonite Community, the church we'd all started. As soon as the other couple came back, and another pastoral couple arrived from America, I must not have felt the need for spiritual direction. I don't remember going back to Manresa House.

But I continued to remember Michael Paul Gallagher's question.

I said it was at a time of great personal need, so why had I gone to a Catholic priest in Ireland for help? We went to Ireland in 1979, my husband and I and another couple, to "model the peace of Christ." I'm quoting from my memory of our prayer folder for Mennonite Board of Missions; it's still difficult after all these years not to be cynical about our idealism and naiveté.

Our assignment was to be the first Mennonite peace presence in Ireland, a country which at that time was still in the throes of "the Troubles," the political violence in Northern Ireland spilling over occasionally into the south where we lived. Unfortunately, our expectation that the violence or lack of peace would be "out there" in Ireland hadn't prepared us for the years of daily strife amongst ourselves as missionaries that followed our arrival.

We were young idealists who had taken seriously the things we were taught at a Mennonite college and seminary. We took the Mennonite concepts of community (by which we meant communal living), discipleship (following Jesus in life), the gospel of peace, martyrdom, and mission on the road, so to speak. We took them out for a spin, living them out with all our hearts, and almost perished in the process. When the communal household ended explosively a few years later, there were relationships and other pieces to try to put back together. One participant has since said that what we hoped would be the "reconciling community" became "hell on earth."

In the process of the community's disintegration, we discovered some gaps in our preparation, gaps in our spiritual formation. (Years later I am more forgiving about those gaps.) We discovered what was missing in the way we had been taught those concepts as we tried to put flesh on these themes from our tradition. One thing missing was a recognition that the human person is more than just something with a commitment-to-discipleship button that is either on or off; human beings are more than a "will." I learned that "a vital spiritual life, not ethical vigilance, . . . makes disciples."[11]

Another thing we learned about was the reality of human sin and brokenness and the need for forgiveness in our own community, not just out there in the world. These had not particularly been "Mennonite" themes in my formative years. We learned about sin and brokenness from living in a communal household, from trying to be fully communitarian, from living under a single roof. This sounds like our spiritual formation didn't teach us anything about forgiveness—I think it did—but the focus was on people out there.

I wrote in the WMSC *Voice* magazine that

> Part of the story of our community involves a complicated saga of communal living arrangements. We began in Ireland as a communal household. Gradually people moved out . . . until today the household consists of one person. In the process, the original core group of my husband Paul and I [sic], Mike Garde and Joseph and Linda Liechty, have gone, and are going through some intense personal changes and growth. We learned we expected an awful lot of ourselves and each other. We learned about the importance of the inner life, about the connection between our witness in the world and our own personal healing.

"We are gradually learning how to be supportive of each other," I continued,

> rather than just committed to an ideal of community. We want to pay attention to the actual relationships among us and not just to the form of community. Hopefully we will learn from our attempt to force ourselves and each other into a mold that wasn't necessarily right in the first place.[12]

In those years, I was angry at my tradition because I felt it had thrown me to the wolves. I felt I had been inadequately prepared for what happened to me in the first five years in Ireland by my upbringing, my education, my tradition: 1) I was inadequately prepared by my seminary education to be a woman in ministry, i.e. both a mother and a church person;[13] 2) I was inadequately prepared to deal with the conflicts and personal issues that arose in our community, having been taught an idealized version of the Sermon on the Mount in which conflict was absent; 3) I was inadequately prepared to look after myself, having only been schooled in self-denial; 4) I was inadequately prepared to be both a family member and missionary and to strike the right balance.

My first silent retreat experience came amid this anger and amid the breakdown of our communal living arrangement and one of the relationships in particular. It came amid the agony and ecstasy of becoming a mother for the first time and doing this all very far from home. It came after seeing the film "Gandhi" and realizing what our constant talk as Mennonites in Irish peace circles about "the cross" might really mean—non-retaliation and willingness to suffer violence at times. It came amid living in the inner city of Dublin which had a reputation for drug-related violence. I was often a little on edge—we were mostly safe because people knew us, but our house was broken into once and cars were stolen outside our house and visitors to our community robbed; and there were other difficulties.

In retrospect now it seems like God was calling me through all those experiences, calling me to trust and know God better. I began to experience a desperate need for a more meaningful prayer life, a deeper spirituality, a closer connection to God, and I had my first retreat experience in 1983. This retreat opened up a whole world of Catholic spiritual formation opportunities that fed me for the next twenty-five years. I describe this retreat in a later chapter. The question of what Mennonite spirituality is, what its strengths and deficiencies are—as compared to the ninety-six percent Catholic culture I was in—became an existential question for me in the total of twelve years I was in Ireland.

Much to my surprise, in 1991 when we returned to America, I discovered that something similar had happened to many others in my denomination.[14] There was some kind of internal logic in this that I wanted to explore. That's why the topic matters to me.

Tilden Edwards says in his book *Spiritual Friend* that we each come from a "deep tradition," and that this deep tradition, this

> tested lineage of experience and interpretation concerning our purpose and liberating way through life is what shapes our innermost being and offering to others. Though we live in an experiential time of transitional and 'broken open' inheritance, *the value of mutating a particular tradition into the future*, enriched and chastened by

other deep great traditions, current knowledge, and historical situation, *is greater than abandoning all traditions and attempting to build from scratch. . .* [italics mine].[15]

In the spiritual search that developed out of my experiences in Ireland, I became aware of wanting to help mutate the Mennonite tradition into this century, "chastened and enriched" by other deep traditions, such as Irish Catholicism, and by the deep spiritual hunger in our new historical situation, but growing out of my own life and thought. I think what I began looking for was the inner life of the sixteenth-century Anabaptists—what helped them face the persecution and the martyrdom? Where was the spiritual experience that buttressed all that? How did they seem so joyful while being burned at the stake or tortured or drowned, often leaving children behind?

I knew I must have missed something as I had learned about them, because now that I was amid the "fiery furnace" I knew that a head-level commitment to nonviolence was not enough. Not for me, not for them. I knew there was something else that sustained them that I hadn't experienced yet. I began to wonder about Jesus' inner life. I remembered the Scripture that tells us Jesus "for the sake of the joy that was set before him, endured the cross. . . " (Heb. 12:2). I was aware I hadn't a clue what that joy was.

I determined to someday study Mennonite spirituality, and in 1998 I started a D.Min. program at Lancaster Theological Seminary to do that. As I formulated my question and proposal for study, I decided that much had been written already about Mennonite spirituality in an abstract way and mostly by men. I wanted to write about it in a narrative way. And I wanted to write about it from a woman's point of view. At the same time my ninety-year-old Mennonite grandmother was very anxious to talk to me about her life. I knew she didn't have long to live. She kept asking me to record her memories, and gradually it dawned on me—that was how I'd do my thesis, by writing about her! I'd look at her life to see how we used to live out Mennonite spirituality, then contrast that to now. So what follows next is the story of her life.

At this point, I need to identify that she is not representative of all North American Mennonite groups. The story of my grandmother that follows is primarily about the Swiss-German Mennonite tradition and the eastern Pennsylvanian manifestation of the tradition that shaped her and me.

I also need to say that there are many American and Canadian Mennonites who have not lived out this same narrative of farm-upbringing that my grandmother did. These are newer Mennonites who won't even know what I'm talking about, because they grew up in cities, or in Latin America, Africa, Asia, or elsewhere. However, when one reads the obituaries in the Mennonite denominational magazine, it is amazing to me that the great majority of them *are* narratives similar to my grandmother's. In fact, one of the reasons to write this book noticing this farm narrative is to point out the very different life experience some Mennonites have had—for example, those from different ethnic groups or part of different generations, including my own. A friend who came from a General Conference Mennonite background said this story of my grandmother was definitely not her experience, but reading about my grandmother helped her understand better where many Mennonites are coming from.

a mennonite
WOMAN

Chapter One

THE LIFE OF SUSAN RUTH (1909-2005)

My grandmother signed her name Susan A(lderfer) Ruth. She was born in 1909 and died in 2005. In those years, in an area just north of Philadelphia, Pennsylvania, she led a life representative of what a certain kind of Mennonite spirituality was then[1] and some Amish spirituality remains today. In 2001, I decided to talk to her and determine what formed her spiritually. I felt I could generalize from her life—discover practices in her life that would help me get at the core of Mennonite spirituality and spiritual formation in the twentieth century.

I wanted to talk to her as well because her farm gave me a sense of being rooted spiritually and emotionally even though I grew up all over the map, in places more urban and suburban. Visits to this farm provided stability for me as I grew up and my family moved around. It was the only place in my childhood that stayed the same. I remember the welcoming yellow porch light as we came down the hill past the village of Lederach that meant they were waiting for us to arrive from Conshohocken or Boston or King of Prussia or Germany or wherever we were living at the time. My life reflects more the disequilibrium experience of many current Mennonites, whereas her farm life represents the older Mennonite spiritual formation model.

During 2001-2002, when I started interviewing her, Susan was ninety-two and her husband Henry Ruth ninety-five.[2] My grandmother told me then that people were always commenting about how she had lived so long. "I wonder why I get so old. Then I think it's so I can pray for my children and grandchildren and great-grandchildren."[3]

When I would visit in 2001-02, I used to find her sitting at her computer—her covering the last vestige of the plain clothes she wore most of her life. (The covering is a white net cap pinned to a Mennonite woman's hair.) Her mind was still active and her e-mail capacity kept her in touch with friends and family. She was almost always the first to the phone—a very sociable person. Her in-service training on computers for the staff at the retirement home where she lived is remembered years later as the best in-service they have ever had.

In another corner of the room in their small apartment at the Souderton Mennonite Home, Henry, whom we always called Pop, preferred listening to the radio and reading. These more old-fashioned pursuits kept him in tune with the latest world developments, however, which continued to amaze and interest him until he died. And his electric wheelchair helped him move around the acres of nursing home where he lived, like he used to travel his farm acres.

A great-granddaughter described Susan this way in a college essay in the year 2000:

> She sits here in her chair, her old-fashioned cardigan over her shoulders, neat covering on her wispy white hair, smiling sweetly, the image of the traditional elderly Mennonite woman. . . . As the visitor's eye takes in her surroundings, however, there are certain anomalies. The electric wheelchair in one corner, the microwave over the sink, the small [musical] keyboard, the computer; these do not quite fit the image of a woman rooted so firmly in the early part of the last century.

"What kind of woman can this be," great-granddaughter Sarah wonders,

> who looks so absolutely fixed in the past and yet has a home with such modern devices as computers and electric wheelchairs? . . . I hope I have an ounce of her strength when I grow old. . . . the strength to keep the things in my past that I value, but to remain open to

change and the ever-increasing pace of technology. There is a space in her head where she manages to keep both the Pennsylvania Dutch [German dialect] of her childhood and the computer literacy of the time she now lives in. . . . She is to me a living emblem of the way the future and the past can combine harmoniously.[4]

What kind of woman can this be, indeed, and how did she get that way? Her life story includes many years as a farm wife, mothering five children; being a founding member of a mission outpost church; learning Russian (through Russian flash cards tacked above the sink to review while washing dishes). Her life includes a midlife career as a ward clerk and operating room aide at the local Grand View Hospital; work with refugees who came into the area from Germany and Poland after World War II—and all in the context of the plain Mennonite community in which she was born, raised, married and lived all her life. In fact, for the first seventy-eight years of her life, she lived on the farm where she was born.

To get to the house where my grandmother was born, one drives in a long lane, past the old farmhouse where she lived as a married woman (where my brother now lives with his family), past the silo and the place where the barn used to be (later a video studio), to a second white two-family 1800s farmhouse (where my parents and my other brother currently live). This was the house where Susan's parents (I'll call her *Susan* from now on) raised her and four older sons beside the Branch Creek and a large meadow full of cow manure piles and buttercups.

Susan was born here in 1909, into a very homogenous community—mostly Swiss or German Mennonite, along with a few other Protestant groups. Most of Lower Salford township's first settlers were Swiss-descended Mennonites followed by all kinds of Protestants, Dunkers, and Schwenkfelders.[5]

The community was quite a stable one, and the farm where she was born had belonged to her family for five generations. My grandmother's early memories are of life in this double-family house, surrounded by extended family. Like many houses of the time, it had a complete house at one end of the building, and at the other end was a unit for uncles and aunts and her older brothers to move into as they got married.

Susan lived in this house from the time she was born till after she was married, when she moved—though not very far—to the house closer to the road. Having four older brothers and no living sisters (two died at a few weeks old) was a source of disappointment for her—an early unhappy memory she told me about at length. The second baby girl was born after Susan, so she got to know her briefly and remembered someone combing the baby's hair after death.

One of her early positive memories is about music, which proved crucial in Susan's life.

> Uncle Elmer . . . had, in the living room there, a little organ, and he would play songs and I would sing. I think I remember that. I guess that sounded something! . . . Me singing. That little "Dutch" girl, you know. I was maybe four or five then.

Susan grew up speaking only German in her family—a dialect of German called Pennsylvania Dutch. She didn't learn English until she went to school. "I don't know how I made out in school the first year," she said. She reported that school was in "English . . . the teacher certainly was English, and we were little 'Dutch' [children]."

The use of a different language distinguished her from her neighbors in the early part of the twentieth century. The early sense of being different in such an obvious way shaped my grandmother's life experience profoundly. There was even perhaps a sense of shame in it. As I talked to her on the tape recorder and then occasionally played it back, she kept saying, "Oh, I hear my 'Dutch' so!" She relates one story about a visit to an English-speaking relative in the nearby town of Lansdale.

> I loved German. . . . I'd be embarrassed to hear it but I wonder what it sounded like [when I first talked English]. . . . I remember we were visiting my mother's uncle, and his granddaughter. . . . and they lived in Lansdale and she couldn't talk that "Dutch," and I didn't understand her. I remember that so well. . . . She was talking and I couldn't understand her. . . . so I must not have been going to school yet. . . . It made an impression on me!

Church services were in High German. The Bible was in High German. The pastors preached in German. Local Mennonites didn't know English when Susan was small, so essentially home and religion were conducted in the German or in the Pennsylvania Dutch language.

Many times in our conversation I heard about how she loved books as a child—indeed throughout her life. She mentioned someone buying her a ten-cent paperback book when she was a girl that was read over and over again. "Books were not plentiful at all," she told me. The Mennonite community at that time (1920s) thought education past the eighth grade was unnecessary, much as the Amish do now. Though she could not be educated past eighth grade, she continued to read voraciously. When we would talk about why I kept going on in school, she would wonder if I liked studying and how many years I was in seminary. Then she would say, enviously, "To think, I was not allowed to go to high school! And look at my granddaughter! . . . See, I used to read, read, read, read, read. . . ."

Susan wrote her own memories in the following piece which she called "Memories of My Father":

> My father was a tall, rather heavy-set man with gray hair ever since I was around. For many years when I would think of God, I would see Him as looking like my father. Or even as the Patriarch Abraham, that being my father's name also. Could it have been that he was a lot like God in my estimation? One of the first things that comes to my mind when I think of my father is his generosity. If someone needed a loan, they would come to him. I don't recall anyone ever being refused. It probably never all came back. In fact I know that in a certain case thousands of dollars did not come back. On two occasions when farmers' barns burned down after being struck by lightning, he gave them each a horse. When someone needed a job, it seemed he always gave them work. Day laborers they called them then. One was a carpenter, another helped with the corn husking and so on and on. How well I remember the *long* table in the dining room with me sitting next to my father at one end

of the table and it was lined on all sides with possibly four brothers, an uncle, my grandmother Alderfer who lived with us till she died when I was fourteen years old, a peddler [Abe Levinson]. Maybe a sister-in-law, day laborers and so on. They enjoyed my mother's good cooking. We would say grace before and after each meal.

My son told me that my father told him someone borrowed his corn planter one time. He didn't return it, so my father bought another one. He also told him that when my oldest brother got married, he asked a carpenter to build several rooms on to our already large farm house. The carpenter replied, "*Ich hab ken leit*" (I don't have any help). My father said "No problem. *Ich shick die leit*" (I'll send the people), and he did.

When my father went to town with his horse and buggy he would often bring something for me, possibly an orange. On one such occasion when I came out to meet him, his horse named Billy, who just seemed to be unable to stand still, moved and the wheel of the buggy ran over me and I was unconscious for awhile. Another time my cousin Ada's family were visiting at our house. She had been stricken with polio and was supposed to do exercises. I don't remember how old she was— maybe ten years. I was a few years younger than she. She was supposed to do exercises. It was probably painful and she didn't want to do this. So my father told her if she would do her exercises he would buy a doll for her. He went to market in Philadelphia and so he bought her a beautiful doll—and one for me also.[6]

In these stories of her father and mother, one can see Susan's soul being shaped by themes such as hospitality—to extended family members and to others, including tramps and the local peddler who joined them at their own table; self-sacrifice or yieldedness or *Gelassenheit*—in her father's loaning of farm equipment that sometimes was never returned; generosity—in her father's loaning of money, never refusing anyone, and his buying of a doll for a relative with polio; gratitude for her father's small and large gifts which she still remembers after all these years. This could be seen as her formation in a nutshell—watching her father and the way he acted in community. Here she learned what God "looked" like. She specifically says, "For many years when I would think of God, I would see him as looking like my father." For her, God was generous, loving, inspiring gratitude, hospitable, self-sacrificial.

Work shaped the rhythm of life. (Mennonites in the early twentieth century emphasized work even as a leisure culture began to grow up around them.) For instance, Susan said her mother always baked all day Friday, in preparation for the more leisurely weekend, when they would celebrate by eating the pies baked on Friday. Company would often be expected on Saturday evening or Sunday noon, so the food would be shared. There was always work to be done on the farm, shaped by seasonal tasks and requirements. Women's and men's work was of equal importance, and the family worked and ate together on a daily basis.

At one point in the interviews Susan mentioned that her older brother had to take care of her one whole summer, when she was still a baby in the cradle, because her mother had to work. Women's work around the farm was valued as much as the men's. She reported that her mother "had to work. . . . helping with everything! . . . She loved to get the meat ready" for market. "Little Susan worked too, gathering bouquets of flowers they sold at market in Philadelphia.

Susan's account of her father continues:

> My father liked to work. He would get up early in the morning and helped to milk the cows. He had strong hands and my husband who was the farmer at this later date used to say he could always tell when my father milked the cows the night before. Because of the strength in his hands, it opened the canal where the milk comes out. Tuesday was the day to start getting things ready for market. They would cut up the pork and get it ready to make sausage, scrapple, roasts, etc. to sell in Philadelphia Market at Eighteenth and Ridge Avenue.
>
> But once a year on a Tuesday morning in early May, we had a conference-wide "Mission Meeting." That was a special day not to be missed. The work could wait till after supper.

Also every Mennonite church had Harvest Meetings in the fall of the year. The long pulpit would be lined with ministers from the different Mennonite congregations. Those meetings would be attended also.

One Mother's Day I bought a Bible as a gift to my mother and decided to buy one for [my father] also. I can still see that open Bible lying on the dining room table well worn in the book of Psalms, where I often saw him reading especially in his later years. As I remember, he used a reading glass at the last.

I never heard him pray audibly, but I can still picture him kneeling at his bedside morning and evening. He could not keep a tune but I remember two songs which were his favorites. One was "I am Looking for a City built of God, Where the Many Mansions be." The other—"I Owe the Lord a Morning Song of Gratitude and Praise."

When he was close to eighty-six years old he had a stroke. The doctor did not want him to be sent to the Hospital, so he lingered for a week without being able to talk before he died.

We can see again here some of the values and virtues that shaped Mennonites' lives in this era and this place. Private prayer was a key value and practice. Susan learned by watching her father pray twice a day on his knees—"morning and evening." The Bible, particularly the Psalms, was a source of consolation. The song "I Owe the Lord a Morning Song of Gratitude and Praise" was written by a Mennonite and is still the favorite of many—highlighting gratitude to God again. Though work was crucial and necessary for sustenance, church was so important that work stopped if need be, for special church meetings. And the Sabbath, or Sunday, was a time when work, at least outside-the-house work, stopped.

When the work day was over, Susan remembers (as recorded in her red notebook), "Sitting under Maple tree—evenings—sparrows. . . ." There was a time to rest. Saturday afternoons were less busy for some families in those days. The practice of visiting in each other's homes was central for eastern Pennsylvania Mennonites. Drop-in company was welcome on Saturday night. It was anticipated Sunday afternoon or evening.

Susan writes about "Much visiting—dinners—Grandma lived with us—every one of her 'families' would often come for a good meal on Sunday dinner. Mother was known as a good cook. Still see the long table filled with good food—ham and eggs for a Sunday supper" (from her red notebook). Susan described food and eating together, as some of her most powerful memories. I asked her to describe a typical meal:

> Well, maybe mashed potatoes and some kind of [meat], probably pork, then [my mother] would do a lot of canning—corn, canned corn. . . . and of course . . . [she] did a lot of baking. [There was a hanging shelf in the cellar]. That would be filled up, practically . . . with pies . . . maybe funny cake and shoofly pie and mince pie and all kinds of pie.

A local delicacy was the dandelion wine:

> We used to sit down in the meadow and pick dandelions, my mother and I. Then she would make dandelion wine. It was good. We didn't drink it by the half-glass or anything but then she'd put it in her mince pies.

Not as much shopping for food occurred because so much was grown on the farm. What they couldn't grow, they ordered from the local grocery store and it was delivered, since Susan's mother didn't drive.

Daily life was immersed in nature, so much taken for granted that Susan had to be prodded to remember details of it. Nature was a given: the meadow where the cows grazed, the creek in the meadow where the family fished, her flower garden. "Pop took pictures of everything else, but not of my flower garden!" Her indoor African violets, even in her retirement home apartment were outrageously productive and flowering—ruffled pink ones, purple ones, with big healthy succulent leaves.

Work shaped life, but daily life was also shaped by the rhythm of nature, by nature's busy productive times, and by nature's lulls. When the hay was ready, one worked until late at night bringing it into the barn. When the winter came, days were shorter and there was not so much work. The rhythms of nature allowed times of intensity and times of mellow restfulness.

As a girl, Susan attended her parents' Mennonite church, Salford Mennonite, founded 1717, about a mile up the road from their farm. She recalls being taken there in a wagon when she was very young and she worshipped there until after she was married. One of the formative practices of her youth was the foot-washing service in which the women of the congregation, in pairs, washed each other's feet, while the men did the same thing in another part of the building. This was done twice a year, in conjunction with communion services.

Another formative practice was nonresistance, or non-participation in war. This was a given, and had been for generations of her family and men in her Mennonite church community. She told me once that she was relieved none of her brothers had to go to war. Although two of her brothers were called in World War I, the war ended before they had to report. By the time of the Second World War, Mennonites had arranged with the Selective Service to do alternate service rather than military service.

Another practice was believer's rather than infant baptism. Susan was baptized and joined the church at age thirteen. She told me why. "I was thirteen and got scared," she reported.

> I guess I thought I was bad, or whatever. One of the [visiting] pastors [from Eastern Mennonite College] said he thought God had a big stick, watching for him to do something wrong. These pastors had meetings at Salford and I thought, *I guess I know what you mean*. I was younger than others when they got baptized. Usually they were seventeen or eighteen. But after I decided to do it, then Sally Weller, a neighbor, decided to, too. And during the baptism, she was crying . . . [O]f course when my parents were young, the [young people] waited till after they were married to get baptized.

For the first years of Susan's life, this church still had preaching in German. The first English preacher started in 1915, although a German preacher continued to preach also until 1936.[7] Susan remembers the first English preacher, Rein Alderfer, who was ordained by lot, as all preachers were, when she was six years old:

> He had no special education at all, and he had umpteen children, and was a farmer, and didn't get paid. . . . [When he preached], he quote[d] Scripture and then he'd say, "Yes," and then he'd quote some more Scripture."Yes." . . . And people talked about him [not in a nice way]. Now I tell this everywhere I go, so maybe I told you this too. So I got serious—they were always so nice to me—[this preacher] and his wife. His wife was my mother's first cousin but that had nothing to do with it. They were always so nice to me; after church they talked to me. And so I got this idea—I'm going to pray for that man! I did, and things changed for me. I still do that on a Sunday morning, if I don't forget it. What a difference it makes for you!

"I got serious" is her terminology for getting serious about her faith. Part of getting serious, in those days, was starting to wear plain clothes.

The "cape" dress was a simple one with an extra layer or cape over the bodice part. It was worn by many American Mennonite women until recent times and was perhaps a carryover from the full cape that used to be worn across the shoulders. Susan grew up in a family whose members wore especially plain clothes, including black stockings, cape dresses, and an apron to hide pregnancies, because an earlier relative was especially "plain" and influenced her mother to be as well.

She says that plain clothes were crucial in her family, perhaps even more so than in other local Mennonite families: "I prayed for Susie and Ruthie [my sisters-in-law] because they let their children wear anklets" instead of stockings.

> And guess what my mother used to do? When I got to be . . . fifteen or so? When she'd buy me . . . she used to buy me nice dress material, at Jonas Landis' . . . store. They had nice material. And then she would buy enough for a cape . . . for me. You know, enough material [to make a cape too] but I didn't wear a cape right away. . . . I had al-

ready joined [the church] but . . . she was waiting for
[me] to say [I] wanted a cape.

I was surprised to learn that the timing of when to put on a
cape was her choice. It was not tied to joining the church.
Maybe it was related to the age when a girl's figure began filling
out. When I checked again on this, Susan repeated that it wasn't
attached to joining the church; it was when one felt one was
ready. The story of her mother hopefully buying extra dress
material when she was fifteen confirms this—but also suggests
it was tied to age.

The prayer veiling was a round gauze head covering ("covering," for short) that fit originally over all a woman's hair
arranged in a bun but got smaller and smaller in the last 100
years, so that finally it perched on top of the head. For Susan, it
still meant a large white covering over the back of her head,
worn every day, with her long hair pulled up into a bun underneath it. It was a symbol for Mennonite women of their being in
prayer, based on the Scripture passage from 1 Corinthians 11:2-
16, particularly verse 5: "any woman who prays or prophesies
with her head unveiled dishonors her head." This passage was
perhaps also the reason why Mennonite Church (MC) women
in eastern Pennsylvania did not cut their hair until the last fifty
years, for it goes on to say in verse 15: "For her hair is given to
her for a covering."[8]

Though the biblical rationale for the head covering (1 Cor.
11:2-16) is interpreted to refer to the "headship" of the man,
Susan never mentioned this as a reason for wearing it. She only
talked about it as prayer symbol for her. Susan commented
about the prayer veiling in her later years:

> When I was working at Grand View [Hospital in my
> fifties and sixties] there was a fellow working there, and
> he asked me why I had this [covering] on all day. . . . And
> I said, "Well, my whole life is a prayer." It just came out
> like that. And I wish it would be!". . . I've been so used to
> [wearing] it since I've been out of school. I wore this
> every day.

I then said, "Every day?" and she said, "Yeah. At home." I
said, "That's right, it's called a prayer veiling, isn't it? . . . That's

what it's supposed to mean. . . . You're praying all the time so you can't take it off. . . . " and she replied, "That's how I feel." To her, it represented a desire to "pray without ceasing."

When Susan got serious about her faith, she also got rid of all her boyfriends.

> And then one night, I had just gotten rid of all my other boyfriends [the night before] . . . the young people used to meet at Souderton Mennonite Church on a Sunday night. And would you believe they asked me that night so I went along. Then when it was over you'd go out on the porch and wait until the guys come up, then you go out! And would you believe, here comes Raymond Kratz with [Henry Ruth whom she calls "Pop"]. Brings him along! And then we went for a ride you know . . . he brought Pop and left his car there, left the Ford, the Model-T . . . stand. Then we went for a little ride and came back. And then I got with him, you know, then he took me home. . . . I'd just turned seventeen. . . . From that time on, until I was almost twenty, we [went together]. . . . Now sometimes we think, why didn't we get married earlier? The trouble was, we would have [had to live at wherever Pop was hired man]."

Henry Ruth, from a farm about twenty miles away, seemed to her differant than other young Mennonite men. He also was "serious" about his faith, as she had decided to be (or soon would), and he wore a plain coat when other Mennonite men his age did not. This inspired Susan to begin wearing a cape dress for the first time. "He wouldn't have made me or anything. It was up to me. But I got real serious then, after I got to know him. And I guess we tried to do what we thought . . . was right."

Susan told me that the other guys she spent time with before Henry came along weren't "serious." After she met Henry, she had an experience one night where she felt she "got saved." "I saw a blue light," she said, "and I didn't want to let it go. A blue light like the heavens. . . . " This seems to have marked a turning point in her life.

The couple waited several years to marry because they had no place to live. Henry's job was as hired man on someone else's farm. One time I heard that Henry thought Susan should go to school while they waited till she got a little older than seventeen. Evidently they didn't think that was old enough to marry. But further schooling didn't happen. Her quote from an older conversation I had with her in 1992: "I loved school and [my mother] didn't. Pop wanted me to go to school, to Eastern Mennonite, because I was only seventeen and he was twenty-one, to take up time till we could get married."

Henry was a hired man on another farm, and they didn't want to live there. Finally, Susan's mother invited the couple to live in her house and Henry could be hired man on Susan's family's farm. Susan describes that moment: "Then my mother stepped in and said, 'Would you like to come up here?' Yes! He ran up here! . . . I think she just wanted me to stay home."

Susan and Henry were married in March 1929, just before Susan's twentieth birthday. Their first child, a boy, was born in early January 1930. In fact, Susan said, "If he wouldn't have been a little late, I always think to myself, people would have thought we had to get married." He was followed by four more children, all girls.

After the second child, they moved out of Susan's parents' house to a rented home of their own at the end of the lane, but Henry continued to be the hired man on the farm of his parents-in-law and later of his brother-in-law all his life, until moving to a retirement home. They never owned their home or the farm.

The nine years following Susan's marriage were a very busy time in her life, during which she gave birth to five children. She reminded me one time, when I said I had had three children and was busy, "And I had five. . . . and the oldest was eight, imagine!"

One interesting illustration of how the young couple, even though they were "serious" about their faith, dealt with the ethos of the surrounding Mennonite community is how they approached the radio. Listening to the radio was frowned on, and broadcasting on the radio was forbidden by local Mennonites at that time. The use of technology and media was considered a threat to community values and was questioned by Mennonites in the early twentieth century, as it is by Amish today. My grandparents upheld the restriction against the radio to their children but used the radio themselves. "It was about five years after we were married in 1929 when we got the radio. We had it hid around somewhere because the people around weren't all in favor of it."[9] One of my aunts remembered how horrified she was as a child when she discovered that her parents did indeed have a forbidden radio. She was concerned for their souls.

Susan's children's health was an issue. She says she still can't forgive someone who had whooping cough and coughed in her baby John's face, giving him whooping cough. Back then one grappled with life-threatening illnesses more often. This more frequent encounter with death was formative for her—she refers often to the fact that God brought her children, as well as herself, through difficult times.

Between her fourth and fifth children, Susan had a miscarriage. She thinks maybe she might have gotten pregnant again too soon after the miscarriage, because her last child, then, was premature. Her memories of this time, when her last baby started coming two months early, are very clear and vivid. She remembers the doctor saying she needed some attention, "or else we'll have a dead baby and a sickly mother."

> That's what [the doctor] said. And I told Pop. Can you imagine how he felt? We had no telephone. It was in 1938. . . . And Pop, he just didn't know where he was going or. . . . He didn't know if I'd die or whatever, you know. And here he had all these children . . . . So the doctor grabbed me and he was just a little guy. . . . Remember those [steep] steps [on our front porch]? He grabbed me and carried me down there, and put me on the back seat [of our car]. And then he said, "Follow me" and took us [led us down in his car] down to the hospital near Norristown. . . . And then the next thing I remember is they took me up to the operating room . . . and it just felt like they were going like this and like this [pulling the baby girl out by C-section]. . . . They brought her in once [afterward], I remember, on a cushion. . . . Here she was, cute as a button!

There was, and continued to be, a keen sense of gratitude to God for the outcome of this dangerous birth (for those times) that resulted in a baby that only had to stay in the hospital five weeks, and a mother who eventually recuperated. She came back to this story often as a sign of God's grace to her.

In those days, Finland, a town in the hills beyond Susan's home in Harleysville, was almost as far away as the developing world is to many of us in North America now. Susan and Henry were part of a mission movement from the early days of their marriage. After marriage, they originally attended the church Henry was from, Line Lexington Mennonite Church.

> Actually I wanted to go to Line Lexington..... where [Henry] was from, because they knew English.... it was so different from Salford! Salford was "Dutch," you know ... [and at Line Lexington] they knew the Bible so well.... So my grandfather—I can still see him sit and talk to me—he said, "If Henry wants to go to Line Lexington, I'd go with him." And that wasn't the case! I [was the one who] wanted to go to Line Lexington!

But about a year later, they were asked to help start a new mission church. The Franconia-area Mennonites were beginning to try to do mission work in local communities and started many "outpost" churches in the years from 1930 to 1955. As Mennonites observed missions both domestic and foreign among neighboring denominations, they began to feel some guilt that they were not obeying that part of Christ's mandate to "go ... and preach, baptizing...." It was a typically Mennonite late response to a spiritual or ecclesiastical current that had been building for nearly a century among Baptists, Methodists, and other evangelicals.[10] Susan described how they were drawn into this movement.

> Clayton Godshall—he went around and asked all these different people.... All these different mission churches started. And he asked [Henry] for us to come to Finland! I guess we thought that was pretty neat! And it was! ... [The town of Finland was so small] they used to say, you go through Finland and then you look back and you'd say, "Oh, there was Finland." ... [We started meeting] in a store building.... It was Mother's Day and I remember the first day better than any other. [I remember all

the other ladies and their children] and me with Johnny
boy sitting on the bench. . . . And that was great.

There was a sense of adventure and new life about these
young couples starting new little churches in those years, incorporating people from the surrounding community who were
not Mennonite:

> The 1930s saw an explosion of mission and social activ-
> ity among the young people of the Franconia Confer-
> ence. Young People's Meeting, prayer meeting, cottage
> meetings, tract distribution, and mission Sunday
> schools became the activity of the day for the restless
> Christian "workers" of the new generation.[11]

Susan and her husband and young family were an important part of this new movement in the 1930s, and she described
it further to me. "The people [of Finland] lived in the hills, and
the stones were so big, you had to kind of avoid them or whatever. And so the people were poor. It was. . . . the Depression, I
guess."

The Ruth family attended here till all the children were
grown. In fact, Susan and Henry attended until they could no
longer drive and were living in a retirement community. Susan
has many stories of helping to pick up people for church at Finland, involving a full car of their own children, plus people
hanging off the side of their car.

> In Sumneytown we picked up Al White. He was black.
> And he was something else. He liked to sing! And then
> he got a friend, not far away, but Danish . . . so we took
> him. . . . Then on the way, Raymond Heitz was walking,
> so he stood on the fender.

It wasn't all adventure, however. There were lengthy revival meetings yearly. "The local Mennonite church authorities,
having resisted the method of evangelistic meetings where an
'invitation' was given, began to bless it after 1930, and for several decades almost made it a New Testament ordinance."[12]
Susan mentioned to me that sometimes the two-week-long revival meetings that met every evening were hard on her family.
These were people who farmed all day and then had to take

young children out in the evening. "And here we had four children," she said, "or five children. . . . And when they came home from school they had to pick up the corn in the fields. . . . And they would milk the cows. . . . And then for two weeks, we would go every night [to the revival meetings]. . . . I don't even want to think about it."

She was not impressed with one of the visiting revivalists from Lancaster County who couldn't seem to remember her name, even though he met her every night. "Every night, he would come and shake hands with me and ask who I was. So I told Pop, then he said, 'Well, you look like everyone else!'"

Susan also became a regular adult women's Sunday school teacher at Finland. She led some more ad-hoc groups at her home, where a mixture of people could freely question, doubt, challenge, search for answers to the questions of faith.[13]

In the 1950s after World War II, many refugees came over from a devastated Europe to find a new home in eastern Pennsylvania. This brought local people like Susan, who had never traveled far from home, in touch with the world in an amazing way. Thus in her adult life we see themes of generosity and hospitality that she learned by observing her father and mother, bearing fruit in her life in a slightly different way—with refugees from World War II.

"[We called them] 'DPs,'" Susan said. "which meant Displaced Persons. It wasn't the nicest thing to say . . . They didn't like it." Local churches, including the Brethren in Christ and Mennonite, would help them get a start in America when they came over.

A local organizer for refugee resettlement was a man in Sumneytown, five miles away from Susan's home. She told me the story of what happened when she was in her forties.

> In [the 1950s], when World War II was over, there were so many people from over there, you know, Germany and Poland and Russia and Czechoslovakia, wherever. There was a man in Sumneytown—we called him a Russian Jew—and he had this furniture factory, and he must have found out about these people, and he kept bringing them over to New York. Anyhow, then [some] of these people who were Polish. . . . somebody [at our

church] paid for them or something, and they started coming to Finland [Church]. And finally they moved to Sumneytown. And so I got interested, because I could understand the German. I could communicate [with them] in German! And, oh my! That was just the beginning. They just came and came and came, until there was no room anymore.

[It was so crowded] they had to wait six weeks [in New York], and then it was like a chicken house. But it was neat.... anyhow, I started to go up there.... I loved languages, you know. And here, guess what? An old [Russian] lady [who knew German].... didn't know English, so she told me to come to her house once a week; she wanted to learn English. ... So she said, "Come to my house.... and we'll read the Bible." ... And then after awhile I thought to myself, Why don't I learn Russian [from her! Then].... I got [Russian] books and stuff.

I remembered the Russian flash cards tacked above her sink, so she could learn Russian while she washed the dishes.

Then there was the couple that had been in Italy ... they were something else.... See, I used to bring them stuff. ... Other people gave me stuff to give to these people. Now it just comes to me what this lady said.... She said, "I never saw such a person like you," you know, because I was helping her and stuff.... they were the ones that drilled me in the Russian language.

Her interest in the people and the language so motivated her that she would be out driving around at all hours of the night. "And one night it got late. It was 11 o'clock. Now, I wouldn't even think of it! But I drove, and on the way.... I got a flat tire. Would you believe I walked down to the garage and the guy came up and helped me." She was only ten miles from home, but it was late enough that she looked back later in amazement at what she had done. Her help included teaching some of the women to drive, teaching English, providing them with donated clothing and household items. Husband Henry would sometimes go along to give haircuts and the

family picked up some of the people to attend their church at
Finland.

The themes of generosity, self-sacrifice, and hospitality
went beyond just helping refugees to actually taking one of
them into her home. Other local Mennonite families also did
this—some building on to their own homes to accommodate
needy people or making do with much less space themselves so
they could fit another family in.

One of the refugee families consisted of an Austrian mother
with fourteen children. When she died in childbirth in nearby
Sumneytown, the children were put out for adoption. Some of
the people at the Finland Mennonite Church took the two sets
of twins. Susan described a later moment:

> Then here was this fifteen year-old [boy], standing
> there, in church you know. [All of a sudden] I just re-
> member standing there [beside him]; I don't know what
> happened. But anyhow, we took him. . . . I can just see
> him standing there.

She turned quiet and reflective as she described this moment when she had found herself standing beside the refugee
boy who needed a home. This Austrian teenager who became
their foster son was named Siegfried Rebnegger.

> And so the last family that came over, Siegfried was
> along with them. It was his real mother but he had step-
> brothers and a sister that they brought along. I think he
> had brothers and sisters they left over there in
> Austria . . . the one brother was taken in by his aunt
> over there. Siegfried wondered: should I or shouldn't I
> come along? Then he came, and he didn't think of the
> language till they were flying over New York. [He
> struggled to learn English.]

Today Siegfried lives with his wife in a nearby town and
still works at the grocery store where he first found a job as a
teenager. He and his wife and grown daughters very much remain members of the extended Henry and Susan Ruth family.

Because of her involvement with Siegfried, the county people knew she could provide a foster home. One time when she

was at work, she got a call that there was a teenage boy needing
desperately to get out of his own home.

> Barry, ai yai yai, that was a sad story. Somebody from
> Norristown called and said, "This boy is climbing the
> walls!" I was working and I just told her I couldn't do it.
> When I came home from work, there she sat with him!
> We were going away, to see the girls, so she said the
> Claude Shislers could take him while we were gone.
> And they did. [So he started to live with us when we got
> back]. He smoked in the house. . . . When we weren't
> there, his buddies would come and gas would get
> stolen. He told us they'd found his father dead.

Barry stayed a few months, then one day his brother came to
get him, and that was it. Another foster boy named Bobby Leis-
ter asked Susan to take him in when his father came to the place
he worked one day and the father really "tore him out" over his
girlfriend. They knew this family from the Finland church. "We
knew the Leisters a longtime. They lived near Lederach and
went to [our] church. Eddie Moyer got them started. Bobby was
such a cute guy when he was little. He had curly hair."

So she asked Siegfried if he would mind sharing a room.
Bobby stayed with them awhile but eventually ran away to
marry his girlfriend.

Grand View Hospital Days

During the refugee years, Susan took a job outside the
home for the first time at age forty-six, at a local hospital named
Grand View. "I got this call from a friend and she was working
in the [hospital] lab, washing bottles . . . and she goes and calls
me [to come work there]. Why she calls me, [I don't know]. . . .
And that's where I was for the next [almost twenty] years."

Eventually husband Henry also got a job there, and Susan
became the ward clerk in the operating room, qualifying for the
job by taking some tests for which she studied out of her daughter's textbooks. "I knew more than the new supervisors sometimes," she said. "Dumb me. I mean, eighth-grader me. You
can't help but learn what you're doing, and I was there a number of years already."

At some point during Susan's years at Grand View Hospital, the stress of having to deal with new supervisors began to tell on her, and she had to quit. She stayed on as a volunteer while Henry continued to work, at the end.

> I think it was '72 when we quit altogether. At the last, I didn't work. I just helped. They gave me a white coat and told me to visit people. . . . I'll tell you how I ended. For five years I put up the tray of instruments, for this and for that [in the operating room]. This was for hernia; this was for whatever. Then the supervisor used to come to the door and she'd say, "Susan" [this and that request]. . . . And then we had another [supervisor] in between there. . . . But I'm talking about before I quit working. The one that was the supervisor then. . . . Oh, she was so nice to me at first. She'd say, "Susan, just tell me if I don't do this right." . . . I'm talking about the last [supervisor]—what kind of got me. Really got me. I had to have her word [at the end of the day] and Pop was waiting [to drive home] . . . and here, she helped the girls put up those trays so they wouldn't get overtime, then they stood around my desk having fun with my supervisor, and I needed her to finish, to help me finish, you know. Oh, I was about [fit to be tied] . . . and that went on for a long time. I finally . . . I quit. . . . So . . . [my] boss asked the doctor if it was her fault. And he said "No." . . . I got sick [you see]. Nerves.

Old Age

I asked her about any regrets she might have had. She said she wished she had done some things differently when her children were growing up. "I enjoyed it. . . . [But] you're so busy, you know. . . . You're so glad when they're growing up, that it's going." She also mentioned that she never really grew up herself, and she talked about how her brothers called her "Madli" (Little Girl) even after she was old, because she was the youngest. This was after I asked her what she would like to go back and do differently with her own children. She said, "Maybe I never grew up."

I asked her about her accomplishments. "Did I have any?" she wondered, and mentioned her children. She often tried to write her life story—there are some half-started attempts in her notebooks, and one time she took a class from her son, a published author, on "writing your own story." She liked what she had written—and her son told her, "This should be pursued," she remembers, but somehow she lost the short manuscript.

In her older age, she enjoyed playing organ and piano for worship at the nursing home where she lived. She was one of the best shuffleboard players well into her eighties. She won spelling bees, mastered the computer, sent e-mail to her children and grandchildren, and once even did the aforementioned in-service training on computers for the staff at the retirement center where she lived.

A tragic event in the 1990s was the death of her middle daughter, who died of breast cancer when in her sixties. Susan and Henry flew out to California, with their son and his wife, to be with this daughter and her family in her last days. "I remember holding her hand while she was dying," Susan told me. "She was such a giving person; every time she'd come, she'd give me sweaters or whatever, you know. And then, about her music—I don't know how many instruments she played!"

I sensed that this was such a sad experience for Susan that she hardly talked about it. The fact that they flew out to California also indicates what a major event this was. Susan and Henry only flew two or three times in their lives, and this was the longest trip they'd ever made. (Another time they flew was when a granddaughter was in a bicycle accident in the Midwest.)

Susan's Faith

Her faith continued to develop in later years. A quote from her diary of February 13, 1993:

Ella Hackman had devotions this morning. She had me up at the microphone too! My contribution was from Romans 10:11, "For the Scripture says, 'Whosoever believeth on him shall not be ashamed.'"[14] Also one of Ralph Malin's "Points for you to ponder" which he always gives at the end of S.S. Meditations "There is no *risk* in *abandoning* ourselves to God." (red notebook diary)

Another diary entry on Jan. 5, 1993 says,

"Home again, Home again, jiggety jig!" That's about the way I felt today after seeing the Dr! There I sat! No temp., no cough—nothing, while he was checking me! I could hardly believe it—and then I remembered—I had asked God to give the Dr. wisdom in diagnosing my condition etc! How soon we forget!

An entry on April 22, 1993:

The Rock Hill Men's Quartet was supposed to have our meeting in the chapel tonight [but didn't all show up]. So [the worship leader] asked [my friend] and me to help the men sing. It was a good feeling, knowing that my strength came from the Lord. I had no time to worry!

She was on a worship committee at the nursing home and encountered people of other denominations on that committee. She was surprised that a man on the worship committee, an Episcopalian, liked the same sermon she did, and she mentioned conversations she had with fellow residents of other denominations about "faith" and "works," an ongoing theological difference Mennonites have with others.

She still struggled as I interviewed her with the "stuff I wish I could forget" about her life. She told me she didn't put any of the "interesting" stuff in her diaries because somebody might read it. She also did not let me tape record some of the things she told me. Her depression was something hard to talk about—the closest she came was to call it "nerves." But she told me about two sermons she especially appreciated by a local pastor who talked about his own depression. He claimed it was our job as Christians to share our life stories, because they are stories of grace, and he shared his in his sermon. She told me about hearing this and how it convinced her to keep talking to me in the interviews, even about the harder things in her life. She especially liked the part where this pastor said, and she quoted this to me: "You *are* a story of God's grace."

Closer to her death, it seemed that having told me the story of her life—including some of the stuff she said she wished she could forget—freed her in an amazing way. At the end she expressed deep gratitude for God's providence. One time when she told me what the doctor said after Carolyn was born, "You have your family now," I sensed how miraculous it was to have had a C-section sixty-some years ago, instead of dying in childbirth. She told other stories of miracles she had experienced. There was a sense of deep gratitude to God, and she repeated several times in our interviews, the lines from the hymn "Amazing Grace": "'Twas grace has brought me safe thus far, and grace will lead me home."

Chapter Two

WHAT FORMED MY GRANDMOTHER?

So then, what have we learned about eastern Pennsylvania Mennonite spirituality, at least in this one life? Susan Ruth's life story stands alone. It was important to me to write it down because I am her granddaughter. I had the urge to help "heal" her life story through having her tell it to me, and the story is simply a good narrative. But it is also instructive. There would be many ways and angles to look at Susan's life to probe its meaning and significance. I especially wanted to look more analytically at what formed my grandmother. What structures or practices formed her spiritually? What was this kind of Mennonite spiritual formation like then? I am hoping that her life can influence our ideas about what's needed now, but first we have to distill the "then." Pardon my metaphor, but often while writing, I had to think of the process of making a good wine—distilling a flavor down to its essence.

A Spirituality of Place

This was very much a spirituality mediated by place, a sense of place. My grandmother made sense of her world through a sense of place in a family system—an extended family—who all lived on the same farm or close by. She lived out of a sense of place in a specific church community—mediated through mutual aid, plain clothes, definite gender roles determining (and valuing) both men's and women's work, and the

German language. She was involved in Salford Mennonite Church from birth to age twenty and only changed church communities once in her life, at the time of her move to Finland church. There was a sense of place in a specific geographical community—the one in which she lived her entire life, not moving once until she moved into a retirement home in her eighties, and her work in this community with Displaced Persons, Siegfried, Grand View Hospital, learning Russian. There was a strong sense of place living close to nature—the Branch Creek, the meadow, her flower garden, the fieldstone house.[1]

We can't help but be struck by the stability of life back then, with this sense of "place" compared to the "displacement" experience normative now.[2] Robert Wuthnow, a researcher of religious trends, describes this:

> A spirituality of place does not simply identify some spaces as sacred and others as profane but has reality by virtue of the fact that people live with a place that is sacred, making it their home, and thus giving meaning to the idea that the sacred is one of habitation (and we might say, of habit and habituation). To live within a spiritual home is to feel that one is secure and that one dwells with God, even to the point of deriving one's identity from being located within this space. . . .[3]

This is the way it was for Mennonite women like my grandmother. It is possible that Mennonites, having been hounded for centuries in Europe, put down very solid roots in America in the eighteenth, nineteenth, and twentieth centuries[4] where the farm could be like a cloister, a sanctuary where they could be separate[5]. The farm was also appropriate because Mennonite spirituality was so much a way of life; it was incarnational—not just abstract or idea or doctrine-oriented, but strong on doing, very earthy, needing to be embodied in the physical.

Delbert Wiens, a Mennonite Brethren professor of humanities and philosophy, describes how these communities formed people. He observes that "The church was the center" of such communities and that

> knowledge and action and faith were integrated by the underlying cultural structure. This structure was ab-

sorbed by the growing child. "Elementary Christian education" [my note: spiritual formation] was the inculcation of this general structure. Since it was always being done, there was little need to set apart special times and places for doing it. It was being done whether the context was religious or not. . . . One then arrived at adulthood having absorbed the structure of the faith.[6]

Spiritual formation happened by a process of absorption— absorbing the structures and practices of honesty, secure family life, marital fidelity, the need for private prayer, the commitment to church, the helping of neighbors—by watching and being a part of the larger Mennonite community. There was not so great a need for explicit formation, because it was being done also by the structures with which one was surrounded. There was Bible study on Sundays, and preaching, which helped with formation, but for my grandmother this was reinforced by what happened the rest of the week.

This spirituality based on place and larger secure structures is not something we can go back to, but we can look at the practices and themes of my grandmother's life and see which hold continuing value and whether they can be mediated by something other than a sense of place. Until recently "Mennonite spirituality was . . . embedded in patterns of life within the Mennonite communities."[7] What were those patterns? Let's get more explicit. Later I will talk about whether those patterns can be made more "portable" into the twenty-first century.

Themes and Practices

Key to my grandmother's spiritual life were the following themes and practices. They include 1) a structure of life that promoted everyday faith, twenty-four hours of faithfulness, a kind of daily sacramentality (often called discipleship or living a life of Christ instead of just going to church); 2) food and eating together with her family three times a day; 3) a special relationship with the Bible; 4) singing and playing hymns and the importance of Pietist hymn lyrics; 5) believers' baptism or voluntarism; 6) *Gelassenheit* or generosity or letting go; 7) church discipline, also called "giving and receiving counsel"; 8) living in rhythm with nature; 9) a particular form of local Mennonite geographical community, which meant that you knew everyone and interacted daily with members of your congregation; 10) mutual aid and visiting; 11) plain clothes/dress, including the prayer veiling, a way to establish a separate "plain" unadorned identity, a way to signal "getting serious" about one's faith as an adult; 12) clear traditional male and female gender roles; 13) a separate language, German, which along with the plain clothes, provided a way to promote separation from evil or from the world, a core Anabaptist value; 14) an emphasis on self-sacrifice, not thinking of one's own needs; 15) living and working on a farm, which meant you worked and lived at the same place, men's and women's work was equally valued, and child-rearing was shared on a daily basis.

Most important of all was the ethos of the community itself, imbibed almost by osmosis, as described by Delbert Wiens, forming a person spiritually into a member of the community, just as novices are formed into monastic communities, but perhaps less consciously.

As in monastic life, too, all of these practices formed a kind of unintentional informal "Rule of Life" (a traditional monastic term). "A 'rule' means the intentional practice of a particular discipline for the purpose of being open to God and [being shaped by that discipline] . . . it is a means by which one can consistently identify and embrace the highest priorities in life."[8]

The "Rule" my grandmother lived was perhaps less intentional than a monastic rule. This is arguable because the plain clothes and obedience to a community set of rules and guidelines was very intentional. Do we now, however, need to be even more intentional?[9] What will replace these patterns? We need to think about and replace the informal, everyday patterns with something more explicit. How will we experience God and live the God-life now? First I want to look at these themes and practices that were key to her life in more depth.

Everyday sacramentality

This was a spirituality of love in action, of love in deed, not just in word. I have started thinking about it as an everyday

sacramentality. I know the word *sacramental* is not one Mennonites have typically used. But Thomas Finger, a Mennonite the-
ologian from Evanston, Illinois, says this in an abstract of a
paper called "How 'Sacramental' Were the Original Anabaptists?" for a June 2003 conference on "Ritual in Anabaptist Communities":

> If *sacramental* be understood in several ways which are
> common today, and also were among historic Anabap-
> tists themselves (ca. 1525-1575), they were anti-sacra-
> mental. But if *sacramental* be understood broadly, as the
> expression of invisible, spiritual grace through visible,
> material channels, historic Anabaptists were very sacra-
> mental. This consisted, above all, in efforts to embody
> divine grace in every activity and relationship.[10]

The following themes and practices are the ways that a
spirituality of love in action was embodied in my grandmother's life—ways that her life *embodied divine grace in [her] activities and relationships.*

Food and eating together
Then they ate three meals a day together; now we struggle
to eat together at all. In contrast to our current practice of sometimes not having time to eat together even once a day, my
grandmother described one of her strongest memories, and it
was of a long dinner table lined on all sides with brothers, parents, an uncle, her grandmother, a peddler, day laborers. This
was an everyday occurrence for her, not a special occasion. She
remembers that this experience was "sanctified," that God was
recognized, by saying grace before and after each meal. (She
told me later that grace was always silent prayer. She never
heard prayer out loud in her family and never could pray very
well out loud herself.)

Arvilla Bechtel, another Franconia Conference Mennonite
woman, born in 1907, two years before my grandmother, describes meals in her memoir called *A Medley of Memories.* She includes many recipes in the back of her memoirs—-for cinna-
mon buns, cheese pie, lemon pie, shoo-fly cake, grape juice[11]—
and gets very specific about meals. "We had meat, potatoes,

and vegetables followed by dessert every dinner, which was
served at noon. . . . We often had sticky buns on Sunday morning."[12] A company dinner was described thus:

> On Friday and Saturday baking was done and pud-
> dings and other desserts were prepared for company. At
> church on Sunday morning, company was often invited
> to go along home with us for dinner, which was eaten at
> noon. [If company came unexpectedly getting a meal
> was no problem] since [there were always] cured hams,
> canned meat and vegetables, and potatoes stored in the
> basement. . . . Company tables set with good china and
> snowy, white, starched tablecloths were beautiful. Dif-
> ferent kinds of pickles and relishes added color to the
> table. Grandma Swartz sometimes made pickled cab-
> bage wedges—coloring one-half with beet juice and the
> one-half with turmeric—and served it in one of her clear
> glass relish dishes.[13]

These meals fed the soul as well as the body. One way they
did this was through the beauty and order which characterized
the table. Women seemed to express their aesthetic sense by setting a colorful table.[14]

Food and eating together, even the presentation of it, created daily sacred moments. God—or the holy—was experienced as embodied, fleshed out, often very generously fleshed
out! You could taste and feel and see it. At a life celebration for
two older women at the Salford Mennonite church named Kass
and Emma Landis, a recipe for chocolate cake was mentioned
several times. And then eating the actual cake afterwards was
just as much a part of the celebration as talking about it! Someone mentioned that Emma's favorite Bible verse was Psalm 34:
8: "O taste and see, that the Lord is good." These ladies often
bake sticky buns and give them to people to celebrate something or to commiserate with them. "Love in the form of sticky
buns" was the way the pastor put it at the celebration for Kass
and Emma.

Another example of the centrality of food, and particular
food, was Susan Frankenfield's (another local Mennonite
woman) funeral. Here a particular recipe for her mince pie was

significant, and there were photographs of her dinner table, filled with sons and in-laws and grandchildren, on display.

Also Mennonites' sending of food for relief—canned beef—overseas, represents the way Mennonites' faith expresses itself in concrete ways. In Ireland, our little community introduced the concept of food instead of alcohol as a focus for parties—the potluck concept. The top Mennonite bestsellers have been cookbooks: *The More-with-Less Cookbook* along with its variations and successors, and the more recent *Fix-It-and-Forget-It* cookbook series for crockpots.

Eating together strengthened the bonds of family and community and provided an outlet for women's sense of beauty. The holy was experienced through taste and smell.

The Bible

The emphasis on the Bible in my grandmother's life was clear. A Bible was the gift she chose to give to her parents. She mentions watching her father with the Bible open to the Psalms, praying, in his later years. Sunday sermons were almost entirely scriptural. Sunday school was basically Bible study. The Bible had a special place in one's life, in the community's life, which was expressed outwardly by carrying the Bible to church every Sunday and by having it on a special stand in the house.

Delbert Wiens describes how the Bible was formative in these kinds of Mennonite communities as their "textbook":

> As far as they were concerned, the Scriptures were written in German. Even those who knew about Greek and Hebrew found that fact profoundly irrelevant. The deeper structures of their way of life provided the principles by which they interpreted, and they simply took for granted that they shared their cultural language with the biblical peoples. Therefore they could all be exegetes and their Bible studies could be completely existential. . . . Because they agreed on the essential structure and on its presence in the Bible, they were free to disagree and to argue. Even in their disagreements each understood the other. They all shared the turf they fought and loved upon. . . . They could discover their

lives IN Scripture because at the same time their lives were being shaped BY Scripture.[15]

This is a huge topic, and I am not a biblical scholar but a pastor. Pastors need to recognize how fully the Bible shaped previous generations of Mennonites as a people. Ray Gingerich, professor at Eastern Mennonite Seminary, noticed at a conference in 2002 that even though the Mennonites there disagreed on many things, they shared the experience of having grown up respecting the Bible and could at least agree on that. They all still "shared the turf they fought and loved upon," as Wiens puts it. For Mennonites not to lose this formative influence, they need to become very intentional about focusing on the Bible, in as many venues as possible. I will come back to this.

Wiens continues: "My grandmother read the Bible through over and over again in her later years. It was her main textbook." He points out that

> No one can avoid being shaped by the shapes he moves among constantly and openly. I believe that she became more profoundly "biblical" than I, though I knew much more about the Bible than she did. The old patterns were limited, but out of them came people whose saintliness must move us to profound humility even as we acknowledge that their road is not for us.[16]

Wiens mentions his grandmother reading the Bible through in her old age. This illustrates that the Bible was used as a devotional tool, not just a study document, perhaps especially when times got harder. Arvilla Bechtel says in her memoirs that when her husband died unexpectedly in his sixties, the "Lord 'gave' [her] the following verse: 'The eternal God is thy refuge, and underneath are the everlasting arms . . . ' Deuteronomy 33:27a.[17] This has been my comfort these twenty-four, plus, years [since he died]."[18] In saying this, she demonstrates a relationship to the Bible which is deeply personal and devotional, beyond "studying." I believe this was representative of my grandmother's generation.

Finally, I need to mention that there has always been a bias toward Jesus' life and the Sermon on the Mount in Mennonites' appreciation for the Bible. That doesn't necessarily come through explicitly in my grandmother's story, but it is there in many sources on Anabaptist spirituality.

Singing, playing hymns, and pietist hymnody

Music was central in my grandmother's life, and what she doesn't say is that the music was almost all hymns. Her early playing of the organ, her later playing of the piano to accompany worship in the retirement home, her citing of hymn lyrics like "Amazing Grace," all point to the fact that hymns pervade her consciousness. Marlene Kropf and Ken Nafziger, in their book called *Singing*, claim that congregational singing is one of the primary forms of prayer for Mennonites.[19] It was also, in my grandmother's life, an important means of formation.

Especially interesting was the role of pietistic hymn lyrics[20] for my grandmother's generation of Mennonite women. This became clear as I researched. These lyrics, reflecting a strong personal piety, did not always fit strict Anabaptist theology but were put to good use by many Mennonites, nevertheless. For example, in "The Spirituality of Ruth Kraybill Souder," an unpublished paper by granddaughter Mary Lou Houser, her two particular favorite hymns are included. These are hymns Mrs. Souder sang on a tape, as a testimony to her faith. One is called "Only in Thee" and the other "He is Mine." Both reflect a strong emphasis on the believer's personal relationship with Jesus.

> Only in Thee, O Saviour mine, dwelleth my soul in peace
>   divine, Peace that the
> world, tho' all combine, never can take from me: Pleasures
>   of earth, so seemingly
> sweet, Fail at the last my longings to meet; Only in Thee my
>   bliss complete, only
> dear Lord, in Thee.[21]

It seems that Mennonites of my grandmother's generation needed to supplement their spiritual diet with pious hymns.

Believers baptism

The importance of being baptized and owning one's faith as an adult—making a conscious choice rather than being baptized as an infant—has always been key for Mennonites. One of the ways the sixteenth-century Anabaptists broke the law, and one reason they were martyred, was because they practiced voluntary adult baptism. In the sixteenth century, when everyone was automatically baptized as an infant, this often involved what others called "rebaptism." The *Mennonite Encyclopedia* explains further in the article called "Baptism":

> Reading the New Testament and finding everywhere baptism tied to repentance and faith, the [sixteenth century Anabaptists] concluded that baptism should not be administered to anyone but believers, and that infant baptism was accordingly no baptism at all but only a *water-bath* . . . [this was consistent with t]heir concept of the church as a voluntary fellowship composed only of those who had an experience of conversion and could intelligently commit themselves to discipleship, holy living and brotherly love. . . [This] was in direct contrast to the prevailing [state] church concept.[22]

This theme, adult choice or "voluntarism," was important in my grandmother's life as she was expected to decide for herself when to be baptized. It was important as her mother waited for her to decide to wear plain clothes and as she herself decided to "get serious" in her late teen years.

Theme of Gelassenheit

The theme of *Gelassenheit*, a German word meaning "letting go" adopted by early Anabaptists, is still carried forward in my grandmother's life.[23] It is best illustrated by her father giving away things that he never got back. I encountered it when I started attending a Mennonite high school, which was my first introduction to Mennonite community. (My family had lived in non-Mennonite communities all my life.) I was shocked when a fellow student in my new Mennonite high school just decided to "let it go" after someone stole the tape deck out of his car. This would never have happened at the public junior high school I had been attending.

The Amish response to Nickel Mines is only understood if one knows this term *Gelassenheit*. In a book which came out shortly after the murders, author John Ruth puts the forgiveness in context. "A neighbor of the Amish at Nickel Mines, when asked how the Amish would react to their terrible loss, replied that while they would grieve, they would have 'more submission' than ordinary folks."[24] This stance of submission to God, also called Gelassenheit or in Pennsylvania Dutch, *Uffgevenes*,[25] allowed them to forgive the attacker and his family from "a stance of yieldedness. . . . [Amish people felt that w]hat has happened needs to be let go, leaving it in trust with God, while hoping always that an evil thing need not be repeated."[26]

In these examples Gelassenheit is a social stance as well as a spiritual stance toward God. It means radical openness to God and others.[27] It is a spiritual-social mix. It begins with God but extends outward into the world through the theme of nonresistance to evil, and non-participation in the military.

Church discipline: giving and receiving counsel

Another theme from my grandmother's life was that of church members being disciplined or spoken to about what was considered sin in their lives. Mennonites have always practiced "giving and receiving counsel"—a commitment upon baptism and receiving church membership, to be open to speaking to and hearing from each other when offenses occur. In my grandmother's day, this manifested itself primarily in the discipline by the bishops. In later chapters, we will look at ways this value can be retained through spiritual disciplines and spiritual friendships, which make discipline more mutual in our currently more egalitarian church structures.

Living closely with nature and nature's rhythm

Another key aspect of my grandmother's life was closeness to nature. She writes in her diaries about going up the hill to see the sunset. Nature was so much with them that she couldn't even verbalize it. Farming created this kind of bond. My grandfather, who was the farmer, was fascinated by nature—electrical storms, the stars (he built himself a telescope), what date the creek froze each year. He even still followed the weather closely in the retirement home through his hundred-first year, although his life was lived almost entirely indoors at that point.

The type of work done was housework, gardening, animal husbandry, and farming, all closely tied to nature. There was some marketing involved, but that was only one day a week, when they went down to Philadelphia to sell their meat and cheese and butter. These types of tasks allowed time to meditate or be reflective. Driving a tractor around a field is vastly different from commuting to work nowadays.

"Mennonites have historically lived close to nature which often resulted in a sense of being and working with God in vocation, community and worship."[28] I want to look later at some of the things that need to change because Mennonites are not as close to nature as they were as agrarian people. For example, I wonder where the following "unhooking" from concerns and worries happens for us now. I found the words of a hymn by an unknown author put to music by a Mennonite farmer, Henry G. Gottshall in 1938. It is entitled: "Out in the Fields with God."

> The little cares that fretted me, I lost them yesterday,
> Among the fields, above the sea, Among the winds at play;
> Among the lowing of the herds, The rustling of the trees:
> Among the singing of the birds, The humming of the bees.
> The foolish fears of what may pass, I cast them all away,
> Among the clover scented grass, Among the new-mown
>   hay;
> Among the rustling of the corn, Where drowsy poppies
>   nod;
> Where ill thoughts die and good are born, Out in the fields
>   with God.[29]

The form of the Christian community

My grandmother was formed by a geographical community of relatives and ethnically similar people, bounded by a twenty-mile radius at the most. "In the past, Mennonites were mostly rural, located in boundaried, solidly Mennonite enclaves . . . individuals and families were usually aware of the needs of other members. It was easier then to think of a Mennonite church as a community, *when it was circumscribed by space.*"[30] I have already discussed the spirituality of place then. This is still the case for Mennonites who have lived all their lives mostly in one place. It also meant that you knew all your neighbors and interacted with members of your church community on a daily basis. Thus people were aware of the daily needs of other members.

Mutual aid and visiting

Mutual aid, very practical mutual aid, was much more possible when one knew one's neighbors' daily needs. This kind of response was expressed in my grandmother's story when her father loaned money and horses to people. The practice of material aid reached out to non-Mennonite neighbors such as the refugees from World War II. My grandmother mentions she took the refugees baby clothes and my grandfather gave them free haircuts. They took children into their homes. It was a very intense, practical caring for people in distress.

This is one of the gifts of Mennonites—their warmth of community, and their spirituality of mutual care. Beth Graybill describes a still-conservative modern-day Mennonite denomination, which resembles what life was like in my grandmother's day:

> The depth of care and warmth of community found in the Eastern Pennsylvania Mennonite Church is uncommon in contemporary society. This sense of community includes frequent visiting at the time of births and marriages; instrumental assistance such as sharing tasks (for example, getting together to can one hundred quarts of peaches), and occasionally financial assistance as well—one Eastern congregation was supporting a young widow to enable her to remain at home full-time with her small children.

Graybill also observes that

> Finally expressions of support during times of tragedy can be especially meaningful, as [a member] describes: "For instance, like when my father died, he died very suddenly of a heart attack and gee, you know, half an hour elapsed, and one neighbor was there bringing folding chairs and setting 'em up because they knew that persons would be coming very shortly and we

probably wouldn't have enough of chairs for everybody that would be showing up. And persons were there with food, and persons came and cooked, . . . and they prepared a meal for the day of the funeral and ah, you know, that kind of thing. It was just there automatically."[31]

This is the sort of practice of mutual aid that Mennonites for centuries have learned by participating and seeing others do it. How can we continue to promote these kinds of face-to-face relationships of transparency and mutual aid and accountability, visiting and mutual aid, when we don't live in neighborhoods anymore and we don't see each other during the week anymore?

The deacons in Mennonite churches used to and still sometimes do coordinate this mutual aid. I still experienced it when our deacon came to our house in 1991 after we returned from being missionaries; she gave us $100 to take a little vacation and told us we could send our daughter to the private Mennonite school for which the church helped to pay.

A member expresses the centrality of mutual aid with the following illustration from the Salford Mennonite church near Philadelphia, Pennsylvania:

Another special occasion in congregational life that will always be remembered by those involved was the replacing of Grace Mininger's barn roof on Thanksgiving Day, November 26, 1981, on Kulp Road, Harleysville. Her husband Walter had passed away that summer, and now she was left to worry about the old barn roof, which was in poor condition. On that frosty morning, many from the congregation gathered at 6:30 a.m. and had the new roof in place by noon. A true Thanksgiving meal followed. Through occasions such as this and others, the congregation has kept alive its centuries-old tradition of "bearing one another's burdens and so fulfilling the Law of Christ."[32]

In my grandmother's day they used to have Sunday church services every other week so they could visit on the free Sunday. Beulah Hostetler remarks about the "frequent visiting"[33] that characterized the late 1800s and early 1900s Mennonites, in her 1977 study of Franconia Conference charter values:

> Fellowship [was] a key value. . . . The practice of hospitality, visiting, especially the sick, sharing in the work and ceremony of funerals—were all considered . . . key. . . . As late as 1937, it was still customary to hold services only every second Sunday. Alternate Sundays were spent in quiet relaxation, Bible reading, and visiting friends and relatives.[34]

She mentions that the Amish still only meet every other Sunday, so they can eat together on alternate Sundays. My grandmother mentioned that at her church they only met every other Sunday when she was a child.

Plain clothes

Plain clothes were crucial in Susan's life—she mentioned the prayer veiling, and the cape in particular. The prayer veiling was a symbol for her of being in prayer. Beth Graybill, a Mennonite researcher, points out that it is the one item of Mennonite clothing that cannot be bought by outsiders. Prayer veilings or coverings are unavailable to buy in stores but can be custom-made by group members.

> The sacredness of the covering extends not only to its purchase but to its wearing and disposal as well. . . . One informant cuts up coverings when they become too old to wear so that outsiders cannot retrieve them and put them to any irreverent use. Moreover, because the symbol is so imbued with sacred meaning, it is not easily laid aside. Dottie, who left the Eastern [Pennsylvania Mennonite] Church ten years ago, still chooses to wear a covering when she goes out to work. As she says, "It's just been so much a part of my life that I can't throw it off abruptly."[35]

I still remember the place where my grandmother kept her covering on a sideboard. I remember watching her putting it on, using little straight pins, in front of the mirror.

The cape dress appears to be tied in my grandmother's life, to "getting serious" about her faith, in her later teenage years.[36]

My grandmother was evidently not ready for this at age thirteen when she was baptized. But something spiritually significant happened for her around the time she gave up all her boyfriends, met her future husband and saw a "blue light that reminded [her] of heaven." This was a turning point in her life, and the symbol for this turning point was putting on the cape.

Other Mennonite women I have talked to have chafed more than my grandmother did against wearing plain clothes. Perhaps it was a more voluntary choice for my grandmother in the 1920s as a late teenager than it was in the case of one of her nieces, Julie Musselman, twenty years later, when much younger children seem to have been required to dress "plain." This sixty-something Franconia Conference woman has written of her battle to get beyond the "external" emphasis she says her Mennonite upbringing in the 1940s and '50s gave her. With the focus on plain clothes, she says, "appearance [was supposed to be] nothing . . . and appearance [was] everything . . . These were . . . the mixed messages Mennonite girls often received from mothers . . . [who were simply] passing on what the church told [them]."[37] Musselman remembers being forced to grow her hair long soon after she entered first grade. She goes on to say, in an essay called "From Anna Baptist and Menno Barbie to Anna Beautiful":

> As my teen years continued, I felt a deepening of the dichotomy between the standards of the church and wanting approval from those who exhibited the worldly standards of beauty trumpeted by the media. My Menno Barbie side was persistently attracted to peers who attended public high school or who weren't Mennonite. Yet I wasn't closed to my Anna Baptist side; I still wanted approval from both adults and peers in my church community whose appearance denoted faithfulness and dedication to those biblical standards of appearance and beauty called nonconformity.[38]

These two women have two very different stories of the symbolic value of plain clothes. It would be interesting to think more about why that is, but one thing we might note is that my grandmother did not attend high school, whereas Musselman did, which perhaps heightened Musselman's peer pressure. I am not sure my grandmother escaped peer pressure, however, since she mentioned that she was one of the only ones among her peers who "got serious."

For better or worse, plain clothes were a formative influence in the lives of Franconia Conference Mennonite women for the first half of the twentieth century. I have chosen to dwell on it at more length than some other factors because it was so heavily stressed at that time. I hope I have given a balanced account. I never had to wear plain clothes, so I hope I haven't romanticized them. I probably would have been annoyed if I had been forced to wear them.

Traditional gender roles

As Mennonites have modernized, one of the major changes has been in the more diversified roles of men and women, given the "equalitarianism in marriage and the development of married women's careers associated with the modernization of Mennonites."[39] However, on a farm such as the one where my grandmother lived, women were not devalued as it is sometimes thought. I did not get the impression from my grandmother that she suffered any lessening of value because of her female role. (Although she did say her mother was more protective of her than she was of her brothers.)

Then, husbands and wives worked together on the farms, and women's work was valued highly, because it contributed much to the overall economic picture. In *Strangers at Home*, one author describes how the Amish farms during the Depression did so well, in contrast to farms where women didn't do so much gardening, preserving, and sewing.[40] On Amish farms there was little the households had to buy with money, since the women made the clothes, grew and canned the food, made soap. This is also how Mennonite farms were in the early and mid-part of the twentieth century, as Arvilla Bechtel describes in her memoirs:

> I did not write much about the busy years of canning
> and freezing food; making soap; tending the chickens;
> grading eggs; milking; cooking for the hired men;
> sewing dresses with capes, slips, nighties, pajamas, cur-

tains, sheets, and coverings; cooking company dinners; tending the garden, truck patch, and yard; attending revival meetings, Harvest meetings, and conferences— since these are in my diaries. It just about makes me tired to read about it now. I know I had quite a lot of "sick" headaches, which was probably due to tension.[41]

Gender roles were very specialized then, whereas now they spread across a wider spectrum of possibilities. Now that women are no longer as available to organize all aspects of family and community life because of paid employment—even as families have less free time than they used to—we need to involve men more in these roles and also find methods of spiritual formation that make sense in these kinds of schedules.

The German language

It is impossible to overestimate the formative influence of having a different language from those around you. This reinforced the concept of "separation from evil," which was also a strong theological theme in my grandmother's day.[42] I learned also that it carried an element of shame with it. ("I hear my 'Dutch' so," my grandmother said when she heard her voice on the tape.) I hadn't realized what a formative influence the German language was for her and for that whole generation of Mennonites. There was the shame mentioned above and also a sense of cultural isolation. The shame was a much more important formative factor than I had realized.

"Separation from evil" or "separation from the world" was a key tenet of the early Anabaptist Schleitheim Confession (1527)[43] and was carried into the nineteenth and twentieth centuries in the Franconia Conference, according to Beulah Hostetler, as "part of [the] basic conceptual framework . . . of Anabaptist-Mennonite belief and practice."[44] The Schleitheim Confession in Article IV, which was called "Separation," "makes clear that this stance of separation was an integral part of the world-view of the Anabaptists from the time of their origin," Hostetler claims. Article IV states:

> We have been united concerning the separation that shall take place from the evil and wickedness which the devil has planted in the world, simply in this; that we

have no fellowship with them, and do not run with them in the confusion of their abominations. . . . Now there is nothing else in the world and all creation than good and evil, believing and unbelieving, darkness and light.[45]

I am making a connection between this theme of separation from the world (or from evil), and the use of the German language up until fairly recently among Franconia Conference Mennonites, noticing that it was easier to maintain this separation when it was a matter of language and almost of an entire separate culture set down amid American culture. However, my grandmother mentioned several times that the families of many of her school friends were not Mennonites, thus "the world" was close by, even then.

One last point regarding the use of the German language: Many of the key terms of Mennonite spirituality are in this first language of early Anabaptists. Sprinkled throughout the current Mennonite Confession of Faith (1995)[46] are words like *Niedrigheit, Gelassenheit, Demut* (lowliness, letting go, humility) which need translation into the languages and cultures we live in now but hold important content.

Self-sacrifice, not thinking of oneself/negotiating conflict

The theme of self-sacrifice was implicit in my grandmother's life, and she is representative of other Mennonites in this. The theme is related, I believe, to the early Anabaptist theme of martyrdom. The necessity of suffering, or being willing to make the sacrifice of one's life to follow Jesus, was a key tenet and experience of early Anabaptists. They were martyred in their thousands in Europe in the early years of the movement for refusing to baptize their children as infants. The stories and pictures of these martyrs were collected in a big book called *The Martyrs' Mirror*.[47] Although martyrdom didn't appear in the interviews with my grandmother because Mennonite were no longer being killed in America in the twentieth century, many Mennonite homes still own a copy of the *Martyrs' Mirror*.[48]

I noticed in my research that the issue of self-sacrifice appeared, although martyrdom didn't. Self-sacrifice arose for my grandmother when she worked at Grand View Hospital. Marcus Smucker describes his struggle with self-sacrifice when he left his Amish background and eventually moved to New York City to go to seminary.[49] I struggled with how to self-preserve when I moved to a difficult living situation in Ireland.

The self-sacrifice mode didn't work out in the non-Mennonite "world" my grandmother had to learn to negotiate for the first time at age forty-six. She needed to learn to fight for her own needs and couldn't, and it got to be too much for her. She had an attack of "nerves" when she couldn't get her supervisor to pay attention to her needs and had to quit her job. Marcus Smucker said he had to learn how to get a seat on the subway in New York. His initial Amish-influenced approach was to let everyone else get on before him, but he soon found that he wasn't getting a ride himself![50] These stories, as well as my own in Ireland, point to the need for new understandings of how the self and others interact, as Smucker says in his 1987 thesis *Self-Sacrifice and Self-Realization*:

> Mennonite attempts to live in community today are spiritually and emotionally demanding in a different way than was true in the past. The creation of the "spiritual community" requires the courage to deal with internal conflict more openly and creatively.[51]

Family life on the farm

The farm was a formative structure that affected the shape of life in so many ways, for Mennonite women like my grandmother. It determined the kind of employment one had—for men, farming; for women, rearing children and helping with farming. One did not commute to a job, but worked and lived on the same property—all of living took place in a particular space. Husband and wife worked in close proximity. Child care was shared, as children grew old enough to help with barn and field work. Physical labor was highly valued. "Work," often bone-wearying work, formed the bedrock of life.

Like the sense of place, this is an aspect of my grandmother's Mennonite life and formation that will probably not be transported into the present, and the differences that makes in our lives, simply need to be recognized.

Conclusion

What most struck me as I researched my grandmother's life is how much has changed. I was expecting to see more continuity between the practices of being Mennonite then and now, and to highlight those continuities. Instead I was more struck by the loss of many of the things that made her who she was.

The form of the local community, the farm, the German language, plain clothes, traditional gender roles, living in rhythm with nature—these have all changed. I was struck repeatedly in my research by how Mennonites live in the vestiges of the Mennonite communal structures and practices that my grandmother experienced. I realized over and over that some of the practices that I still do or observe are leftover ones that previously permeated life. Things I've felt in my bones without knowing why have become clearer.

Her covering, I say, was a "vestige." Many of my instincts are vestigial—not to dress in ways that suggest conspicuous consumption, to do potlucks, especially after a death. Much of what happens at my local Mennonite church is vestigial, like our footwashing service, with women at one end of the church and men at the other; like the *Fastnacht* doughnuts people still make in eastern Pennsylvania on Shrove Tuesday; like the "council meeting" (self-examination connected with twice-yearly communion) still occasionally preached about that hasn't happened for years. It's fragmentary, living in these vestiges. Can we make our experience more whole, explicit, conscious?

Some structures are gone, but much does remain. These themes and values must be articulated and reembodied or they may be lost. Values such as hospitality must now take different forms. Mennonites don't host the local tramps at our dinner table any more, but we can still help with refugee resettlement, for example. I hope we can still be Christian and not be farmers, but what new forms of community will we need? We can still be formed by the Bible, but it will have to be in new and intentional ways. Particular contexts have been lost, but their values need to survive (as I address again in my final chapter). We need to recognize the extent of the loss of old contexts for most Mennonites in the Mennonite church today (urban, non-Western) to fully address our new situation.

Chapter Three

WHAT FORMED ME?

A White American Urban/Suburban Childhood and a Mennonite Subculture

My life has been so different from my grandmother's that my seminary professors, the advisers for my thesis, asked me to check with her about where she saw the commonalities between us. They asked me to find out what she thought we had in common, since our lives went in such different directions. So I asked her one day about where she saw the continuity between her life and mine. She said: "You're just as interested in the Christian life as I am."

So there is continuity, but I want to describe the differences now. Now that I have described her life, I will describe mine a little, because I discovered as I wrote this account of her life that my own life is more normative for a new generation, a different breed of Mennonite, whose lives, like those of many Americans, are more characterized by a sense of displacement than a sense of place—and for whom many of the practices of my grandmother's life have been sporadic and fragmented if not non-existent.

I wore a "covering" or prayer veiling on only three days of my life (and enjoyed it as a symbol of belonging). Since I did not join the Mennonite church until I was twenty, I did not have to wear a covering at the Mennonite high school I attended. Coverings were only required for members of the church. I did wear it for Halloween during one of my teenage years when I dressed up in my grandmother's plain clothes, which I loved to do.

The second time I wore a covering was the day (Dec. 1972) I joined an eastern Pennsylvania church, but then I went back to Indiana, where I was in college and they had long since stopped wearing coverings. And I wore one the day I got married because women wear veils when they get married, and I thought it would make at least as much sense to wear the covering I never had a chance to wear. That was it for me and the covering.

The shape of my life, and others of my generation, has been very different from the one I described in the last two chapters. I didn't grow up on a farm—in fact, I didn't stay in the same place longer than six or seven years growing up—I grew up in Conshohocken, a working-class suburb of Philadelphia, Pennsylvania, where my parents ran a mission church and we frequently drove the fifteen or twenty miles upcountry to visit my grandparents. I also grew up in Boston and Westport, Massachusetts, where we followed my father studying at Harvard University and for two years worshipped with the Quakers.

Then we moved to King of Prussia, another suburb of Philadelphia, where my father taught at a Baptist college and I attended Roberts Elementary and Upper Merion Junior High School. I even spent one of my high school years in Germany. My other three high school years, when I commuted the twenty miles up from King of Prussia every day to attend a Mennonite high school, people thought I was a foreign student at first. And I very much felt like one.

I tried to understand the Pennsylvania Dutch language my grandparents spoke, but I couldn't. In fact, I think they talked this language on purpose sometimes so we couldn't understand what they were saying when we were children and they wanted to have a private conversation.

So rather than experiencing "sacred place," many in my generation and the ones coming after have lived something more like "displacement." Moving from one community to the next is more normal now. A researcher of American spiritual movements, Robert Wuthnow, has described this well. Wuthnow describes two types of spirituality in a book about spirituality in America since the 1950s:

People who enjoy the security of well-established homes and of enduring communities and who live orderly lives with familiar routines and organized roles can imagine that God is indeed in heaven and that the sacred may be worshipped within predefined spaces. People who are faced with a dizzying array of choices and who experience so much uncertainty and change that they must negotiate and renegotiate their relationships, if not their very identities, are likely to find it easier to imagine that the sacred manifests itself at odd times and in less predictable ways. . . . Paying attention to the relative emphasis on dwelling and on seeking, as well as to the social conditions that reinforce these orientations, is thus a way of clarifying how dominant understandings of spirituality have been changing.[1]

Going to market to sell their meat and eggs in Philadelphia was a once-a-week thing for my grandmother's family, but contrast that to our commuting to work every morning sometimes forty or fifty miles. And my commuting northwest to a retreat center fifty miles away for retreats, east twenty-five miles to a suburb of Philadelphia for spiritual direction, west sixty miles to Lancaster for seminary. Wuthnow continues,

There are many ways of experiencing the shift from dwelling to seeking. For some people, the shift is experienced as living no longer within a sacred space but between sacred spaces. At one time, people were residents of their communities; now they are commuters. . . . The same is true of spirituality. At one time, people identified their faith by membership; now they do so increasingly by the search for various organizations, groups, and disciplines, all the while feeling marginal to any particular group or place.[2]

Many of those "well-established homes and enduring communities, orderly lives and familiar routines" Wuthnow refers to, those structures and practices that nurtured my grandmother, are gone. Beulah Hostetler said in her 1977 thesis that "Since about 1950 very rapid acculturation has been taking place in the Franconia Mennonite Conference in Eastern Pennsylvania. Virtually all of the well-known symbols of Pennsylvania Mennonitism have been abandoned in the span of two decades."[3] Thus, according to Hostetler, the symbols of my grandmother's life began to disappear some sixty years ago and were almost completely gone by the 1970s. That means the current generation has grown up largely without them. The shape of life has changed drastically.

We can also say this in more sociological, fact-based terms. The *Mennonite Mosaic: Identity and Modernization* is a book about modern Mennonite-Anabaptist life based on findings from surveys of five Mennonite and Brethren in Christ denominations in 1972 and again in 1989. The surveys attempted to find out the current beliefs, practices, and social attitudes of people in these five denominations. They found more members becoming urban (in 1989 only seven percent of Mennonites were in farming), geographically mobile, and achieving higher educational and socioeconomic status. The authors note that members of these churches cope with increasing pluralism while still retaining their roots in the Anabaptist tradition.[4]

In *Strangers at Home*, in a chapter on Anabaptist women and anti-modernism, Jane Marie Pederson, history professor at the University of Wisconsin, describes the change in these terms:

> In myriad ways, women from the American Anabaptist traditions encapsulate in their lives and thought two centuries of transformation. Because Anabaptists, especially the Old Order Amish, self-consciously chose to resist many of the cultural and economic changes of the dominant society, they now stand on unique ground. *In a single generation these women sometimes move from a premodern social order . . . to the postmodern context of an urban woman.*[5] [my italics]

This is the situation in a nutshell. The life my grandmother lived is gone, for most of us.

In *Practicing Our Faith: A Way of Life for a Searching People*, editors Craig Dystra and Dorothy C. Bass listen to a typical modern American woman describe her life:

> "I never thought I'd be living this way," she says. . . . Too few evenings include nourishing suppers shared with

loved ones; too many are given over to the demands of paid work or housework, or lost to worry and exhaustion. Her closest friends are spread across several time zones. The old neighbors she entrusted with the house key are gone. . . . The sighs of this woman and so many of us today come only in part from having too much to do. Even more, these sighs are born of our yearning to understand what the too-much-to-do adds up to. We long to see our lives whole and to know that they matter. We wonder whether our many activities might ever come together in a way of life that is good for ourselves and others. Does all this activity make a difference beyond ourselves?[6]

My life is very much like the above, and I suspect most of us would say the same thing. In this type of environment, a Sunday morning at church isn't always enough to address the week-long issues, and so I find myself at retreats once a month as well.[7] A Sunday morning at church does address the fragmentation of meaning but not the schedule overload. *Fractured* and *frantic* would be two key words to describe what life is like now.

A spiritual hunger is there in us—a longing for centeredness, for wholeness, for the opposite of fragmentation. And as I said above, I have found these hungers addressed more deeply in retreats than in the institutional church, which often just seems to offer more to do. I have also found these hungers addressed in a spiritual friendship I have with another Mennonite woman, a peer, and in a spiritual direction relationship with an older Quaker woman.

The basic shape of life has changed, necessitating new structures and practices to form and nourish us spiritually. A sense of coherence is gone—that holy sense of place, a spirituality based on place.

When so many of the signposts are gone, we are in the Dark Night.[8] A biblical metaphor that feels like it describes this situation that twenty-first-century North American Christians find themselves in now is the story of the call of Abraham. At age seventy-five, Abraham and Sarah were called to go out from their homes to an unknown place. They moved from a dwelling mode to a seeking mode; from a "place" mode—from their country, their land, and their kindred—to a "pilgrimage" mode. They started on a journey with no known destination—with only the promise of God, the relationship of covenant with God, as reassurance. It sounds inviting and scary.

But I believe it's happening! It's happening to many Mennonites just by living in the modern world. Even if we don't go anywhere, even if we stay in our old communities, we're moving into the unfamiliar, or it's moving into us. The world around us is changing, our children are changing, change is here. We don't really have a choice! But we can choose to understand this as a call from God—and we can choose how we respond to the invitation.

We can bless the world with some of our themes of humility, of generosity, of meekness, of community support and nourishment. In a world that often seems so arrogant, these are important signs of God's upside-down kingdom. I've used my grandmother's life story to describe these familiar blessings that are often so close to us we don't even see them. They're so much a part of us. But I believe our themes of the faith can speak hope into a world filled with war and fear and too many possessions and commitments.

Mission in Inner-City Catholic Ireland, Including My First Spiritual Retreat

I was also formed differently than my grandmother by an extended time of separation from Mennonite community. I learned that our themes of faith can speak hope when I was in Ireland from 1979-1991. I have referred to these twelve years of mission briefly in the introduction and pointed out difficulties and negative experiences we faced. But now I would like to zero in on two of the positively formative experiences of those years, my first retreat experience (where I learned *lectio divina*), and then exchanging visits between an Irish Cistercian monk named Brother Eoin and our little Dublin Mennonite Community. (*Eoin* is Irish for John—pronounced like Owen.)

I will describe my first retreat by drawing on an article I wrote as well as a letter to my parents and my journal. It is amazing to me that even then I must have recognized the importance of this first retreat, because I basically wrote what follows as an article for a magazine. It was never published, but I'm glad I saved it for this book. "What an experience!" were my opening words in an October 1983 letter and also the opening of the article I tried to write.

My first retreat

It was a beautiful fall weekend and the Carmelite Center of Spirituality—also called Avila—is situated in a little oasis of greenery surrounded by Dublin on every side.

My window looked out on the orchard and rows of cabbage and lettuce. Then over the wall was a little street of brick houses with all the normal activities of life going on—people getting into cars and driving off, etc.

I could go on and on about this retreat—the actual physical surroundings, so deathly quiet, and even the toilet doors, which had triangles carved into them so you could meditate on the Trinity, I suppose. I could go on about the Irish nun who revealed at lunch that she had been a missionary in Burma for forty years without one furlough, and for four or five years during the war they got no mail. (This made my own current missionary experience seem like a piece of cake.) I could go on about the whole experience of *'retreat'* from everyday goings-on. In the end I decided being on this retreat was the opposite of a grocery list (the type of activity which comprises much of my life these days). Being on retreat was focused and transcendent rather than fragmented and mundane.

It was the first time I'd been to a spiritual retreat, and I experienced quite a bit of trepidation about it, almost backed out, kept thinking of excuses not to go, like one does going into any strange situation alone: Would there be ladies' restrooms in a male monastery? Would there be anyone else there but me and the monks? Who would I eat with?

I was also worried because it was the first time I'd left my daughter overnight since she was born, almost two years earlier. Sure enough, as she began to realize when we arrived in the parking lot that I was getting out of the car and she wasn't, a wail went up, and it was very loud as I shut the door of the car.

What a feeling of guilt and irresponsibility I had as I saw a group of men getting out of a car a little distance away. What was I doing, going off and leaving a poor defenseless baby for a weekend? At least that's what I imagined the group of men thinking as I shut the car door on a screaming baby.

A monk took me up to my room. We passed a poster of a bulldog that said, "Lord, Save Us from Sour-Faced Saints." That was reassuring! We went through heavy wooden doors and long corridors and up wide, brown-carpeted stairs to my little cell. What quiet there was! Little signs were posted: "QUIET." And indeed there was a feeling of quiet and a lack of activity.

I was still very agitated about leaving my daughter, and I decided to phone home right away to see if she'd ever stopped crying. The pay phone near the front door seemed crucial—a lifeline to the outside world. A feeling of panic began to come over me: What if we're trapped inside this place, locked in? A feeling of being totally cut off from the world and my family. But sure enough, the phone did work, and I found out Sarah had gone to sleep.

In the first session, there was a whole roomful of people, mostly nuns, a few sheepish-looking men. Our leader came in, wearing brown robes, looking like death warmed over. His skeletal ascetic look reinforced my feeling of death.

My journal said that "Evening prayers are also very oriented toward death. Night is closing in. I've never been in a gathering of people willing to look at their own death together. Maybe no one else noticed."

Then into my room. Back to make another phone call—one last desperate attempt to make contact with the world. I told Paul which number to ring in the middle of the night if Sarah needed me. Back again to my quiet, orderly room. A dreadful sensation of loneliness, anxiety, only partly allayed by the sight of a Cadbury's chocolate bar I had brought along and the sight of my familiar clothes. Why was it so hard for me to be alone?

Journal: "The leader tonight was talking about faith being essentially trust. That's a good point to make for me. But then he started using the example of little children in their mother's arms as an example of trust, and I began to worry about my daughter. I worried that I'd ruined her ability to trust in one night, by going away. Then later I had a kind of feeling that God was planning to look after her, not specifically tonight but generally."

There were some nut trees on the walkway I took many times around the grounds that weekend. Our retreat leader compared reading a passage of Scripture once with picking a nut. Only as you read it twice, three times, four times, do you begin to get into the nut, like a squirrel turning a nut around and around as it nibbles. We learned about ruminating on Scripture, reminiscing about other Scripture it brings to mind, imagining ourselves as Mary Magdalene or others in the story, and experiencing it as if it happened to us, which he called "memory." Later I realized he'd been teaching *lectio divina*.

I wrote to my parents: "A weekend like this makes you realize how much noise there is in community, or perhaps in any ordinary life. 'Exterior and interior silence is the beginning of purity of heart,' according to St. Basil."[9]

I read a book while I was there called *Prayer of the Heart* by George Maloney. One afternoon I journaled about having read a sentence that summed up what I was often feeling when pregnant, indicating that "integration begins as we let go of the controlled consciousness that we hold over our lives and surrender in complete poverty to God's gift of himself as grace."[10]

In the journal I continued, "I don't think it's an accident that the person who symbolizes total trust and obedience to God's will is pregnant in the Bible. It's hard to maintain 'control' when a new being is taking over your body in pregnancy. Maloney calls this attitude of complete surrender 'the heart of Mary.'"[11]

This weekend in a strange setting apart from my husband and child feels very much like what Paul Tillich calls "the anxiety of non-being." Maloney says, "It is this anxiety and fear of letting go of our 'linus blanket' of pseudo-security that we all resist in the beginning stages of a conversion of ourselves toward God and toward our true person in His Word. To split this hard shell of self-containment and control over ourselves, over others and over God is the harrowing first step into new life."[12] This "splitting the hard shell" is what pregnancy began to do to me.

Do I always search for diversion, do we always search for diversion to shield ourselves from a sense of emptiness? Maloney continues to observe that "through this emptiness we inevitably become aware of the misery of our condition, a condition so miserable . . . that nothing can console us when we think about it carefully. Hence the necessity of diversion."[13]

By the end of the retreat I had become a little more used to the emptiness. The quote I used in a letter home to sum up my experience was this: "To live a spiritual life we must first find the courage to enter into the desert of our loneliness and to change it by gentle and persistent efforts into a garden of solitude."[14]

Meeting Brother Eoin De Bhaldraithe

The other major formative experience I had in Ireland was meeting Brother Eoin. I wrote about this first encounter with Bro. Eoin for our denominational magazine during that period,[15] so I will draw extensively from that article. At the time of this visit, we were frantically trying to build a church meeting place in the basement of the house where our intentional community was living, all the while actually living in it. I remember being desperate to find time amid my responsibilities of cleaning and cooking and babysitting for a crew of builders to sit down and reflect on this visit in the form of writing an article. So even at the time it happened, I must have been very influenced by it.

I also wrote about Bro. Eoin in a sermon on "mission as reciprocal hospitality" that I preached in about ten different places after we came back to America. I realized more and more after the Ireland part of my life was over that we learn from each other when we're sent out in mission. When I met Bro. Eoin I felt like God sent me to Ireland to learn from Catholics, particularly his tradition which had some of the best of ours— but also some ingredients ours was missing: prayer as undergirding and the importance of silence.

I was struck at the time by all the commonalities I noticed between his community and ours and didn't know *why*—I didn't know the historical connections, at the time. Now I know that a shaper of sixteenth-century early Anabaptism, Michael Sattler, was originally a Benedictine monk. Some scholars feel Anabaptism has links to ascetic Catholic movements such as the Benedictines. Cistercians were a reform movement in the Benedictine tradition. But I figured that all out later.[16] These are the words I wrote at the time.

The weekend of May 9-11, in the year 1980, while living in Ireland, Mike Garde, Paul my husband, and I followed up an invitation to visit a Cistercian monk at Bolton Abbey, named Brother Eoin de Bhaldraithe. We knew nothing about the Cistercians, just that they were a small monastic community of farmers about forty miles south of Dublin in Moone, near Athy, County Kildare. We took the bus down and Bro. Eoin picked us up in a car at the bus stop. I'd never met a monk before that I could remember.

We'd gotten into contact with Bro. Eoin de Bhaldraithe through reading an article he had written called "All Who Take the Sword: The Pope on Violence" in *Doctrine and Life,* an Irish Catholic journal.[17] After examining Pope John Paul II's speech given during his visit to Ireland in 1979, Br. Eoin concluded in the article that a Christian cannot be involved in any kind of violence, revolutionary or state-sanctioned. He quoted from John Howard Yoder's *The Politics of Jesus* and gave evidence that early church fathers assumed all murder was grounds for excommunication. His conclusion was that "the just war and pacifist theories are not just two options, to either of which a Christian may freely subscribe. Rather the ideal of Jesus is 'to accept the ultimate violence of death rather than do violence to a fellowman.'"

Bro. Eoin had written not only this article but also a letter to John Howard Yoder, giving him a copy of it. He knew Yoder only from having read *The Politics of Jesus.* Yoder, in turn, contacted us because we'd had dinner with him before we went to Ireland to tell him what we were trying to do (live out his little booklet called *As You Go*). Yoder wrote and encouraged us to go visit Bro. Eoin, so we did.

Our first visit turned out to be one long, continuous conversation with Bro. Eoin, punctuated at intervals by the different elements of his monastic day. When we asked how long he could talk with us, he replied, "Well, I have to feed the calves at 4:30." This was his task on the monks' 280-acre dairy farm. Bro. Eoin would go to bed about an hour after 8 o'clock vespers. The monks begin their day with a morning mass around 5 a.m. By the time we got up, Bro. Eoin would have most of his work done for the day, and we could talk until the monks said another office and ate lunch shortly before noon.

Bro. Eoin would take a short nap after lunch. "It's a habit we developed because our order originated in France," he explained. "I think a half hour after lunch is better than an extra hour at night." When he woke up, we could talk again until he had to feed the calves and say another office before supper. Somewhere he must have fit in some sacred reading, because that is another important element in the carefully balanced day of a Cistercian monk: equal parts manual labor, sacred study, silent meditation, and liturgical prayer.

Bro. Eoin told us the first evening that he preferred to be called brother instead of father, although he is ordained as a priest. He wore a worn-out overcoat the entire weekend; he claimed to be wearing it because he had a cold. I wondered if he was wearing it to minimize the difference between us, so that we wouldn't be alienated by his special clothes underneath. (He wore a long white gown with a black kind of apron over it back and front, fastened together by a huge leather belt.) It would have been consistent with his desire to be called brother not to look so different from us.

We learned of his early biblical training under a self-educated man who played down the importance of "traditions" surrounding biblical texts and stressed the importance of doing what Jesus commanded. Br. Eoin also studied the early church fathers during several years of training in Rome. He chose to study the period of the early church over medieval or Counter-Reformation theology because it was closer to Jesus, he said. We felt we had met a Christian who had come to conclusions similar to ours without benefit of knowing the Anabaptist tradition. We talked and talked.

Of course, he and Mike had their own conversation on the political scene in Ireland and how the Christian should relate to it. Bro. Eoin informed us that he had decided against joining the Irish Republican Army (IRA) just before entering the monastery. Mike calls himself a Republican (advocating a united Ireland though not violently like the IRA), so they had a lot to say.

Paul asked Bro. Eoin how he had come to the conclusions on nonviolence he expressed in his article. He attributed it to his experience of living in the monastery, of being a monk. A Cistercian is encouraged to read the New Testament each day. Gradually reading through the Gospels and especially the Sermon on the Mount in *lectio divina*-style led Bro. Eoin to the conviction that Jesus preached a gospel of love that prohibits violence. The experience of living in a close-knit monastic community and trying to apply Jesus' words to relationships with the brothers also developed his convictions. "There are always those people in any community who are not as easy to like as others," he said. "I try to love and turn the other cheek to all the brothers here, as Jesus taught us. I just applied the principles I found important in the monastic community to the wider community and then to the national struggle in Ireland."

Bro. Eoin has strong feelings about the hatred Catholics feel toward Protestants in Ireland. The basic problem, he believes, is that "there's just a deep feeling that the Northern Protestant doesn't belong in our country." Although he feels most Catholics would agree in principle with what he says about Jesus' preaching on love, "The next day they'd still be glad when they heard another Loyalist [Protestant] had been killed." Bro. Eoin feels his mission is to change the Catholic community—seeing the "Irish problem" as very much a "church" problem.

I was struck over and over by the many common elements in the Cistercian and Mennonite traditions, apart from the fact that this particular man was perhaps closer to us than most of the other brothers. Their view of the "world" is similar to that of the Amish, and separation from the world has motivated these monastic groups since the church first became confused with the broader (unfaithful) society. A quote from a booklet on Cistercian life says, "Separation from the world demands that journeys out of the monastery should be infrequent and only for se-

rious reasons. The use of radio and television will be excep-
tional. Discretion is needed in the use of other media of com-
munication."

The theme of humility is also crucial in the Cistercian community. Another quote from the booklet: "The monastery
teaches men to take their own measure and to accept their ordi-
nariness; in a word, it teaches them that truth about themselves
which is known as 'humility.'" Bro. Eoin explained to us that no
one does the same job at Bolton Abbey for longer than a few
years. "I used to do the milking, then I was switched to feeding
the calves," he said somewhat sadly. They do this to prevent
anyone from feeling possessive toward a particular task, and
they stress that people who are over-ambitious would find their
way of life very difficult.

There is a strong emphasis on community and sharing of
goods in the Cistercians. They claim their ideal is to be like the
first disciples in Jerusalem, who held everything in common.
Each monk has his task which contributes to the life of the farming community and the hospitality they offer. I was interested
to note that there was not a maid or cleaning lady around the
place, even though they have a large guesthouse as part of their
ministry. The monks do all the work, including what is usually
identified as the "women's work." The monks hope that because of their way of life, people will identify them as disciples
of Christ.

The order is based on the foundation of New Testament discipleship. Their introductory pamphlet says, "Our aim is very
simple: we are disciples of Jesus Christ and strive to live according to His gospel. Everything else is secondary to this great
ideal which is common to all Christians."

And there is also inherent in monasticism a critique of
Christendom and participation in violence, according to Bro.
Eoin, similar to the Anabaptists. Bro. Eoin was doing research
when we first met him to determine whether the monastic vow
of obedience was originally a vow to "turn the other cheek" in
all human relationships.

At the time of my first visit I was still sorting things out; I
said there were many differences between our two traditions as
well. Some of these, I said, could be helpful to us, others we

question. Their emphasis on liturgical prayer could nurture our community, and we could certainly learn from their stance on celibacy, although we aren't quite sure how. But we felt uneasy about their attitude toward the laity, making a distinction between monks and "ordinary Christians." Bro. Eoin himself did not make us feel uneasy, but we worried about whether there was a sense of coldness toward the neighboring Catholics who attended the monks' mass on Sunday mornings. This distinction between the "religious" (those who profess monastic vows) and the laity is not much different, however, from the Mennonite attitude that our way of life is right for us even as not everyone is called to it.

Bro Eoin's attitude toward the pope was interesting. In the article that first drew our attention in an Irish periodical called *Doctrine and Life*, he said he wanted to compare what Pope John Paul II said during his visit to Ireland in 1979 with the pacifist position and see how the pope measured up. He used the opportunity of examining the pope's speeches on violence to say things he had wanted to say for a long time.

> Obviously I was glad when the Pope came along and agreed with me, though maybe his theology isn't quite as strong as I've described it. For years, I was hoping for a chance to put forward these views, but my voice alone wouldn't have carried any weight.
>
> I really wrote this article as a challenge to the pope, showing him logical next steps. For instance I say at one point, "The Pope has nothing to say on the demonic nature of power." That's straight from John Howard Yoder. I thought if the Pope read that he would say, "Hmm . . . next time I'll have to say something on the demonic nature of power." I sent the article on to the pope and I know it got through to him.

We agreed in 1980 after our first visit to keep in contact with Bro. Eoin. He put a notice in an inter-Cistercian newssheet about the Mennonites and our willingness to visit other communities. Nothing ever came of that, but we did continue to visit back and forth with Bro. Eoin for the rest of our years in Ireland, and he began to meet other Mennonites. He found out about Michael Sattler, as I mentioned above, the Benedictine monk who became a leading founder of the Mennonites, and began exploring more parallels between our two movements.

Bro. Eoin came to the U.S. several times on speaking engagements. One of those times he attended a Mennonite church[18] and apologized publicly in the worship service for the persecution of Mennonites by Catholics in the sixteenth century. Bro. Eoin also served for many years on an advisory board on Mennonite mission efforts in Ireland. The relationship between Bro. Eoin as Cistercian and the Mennonites continues to develop even now.

In a sermon I wrote in 1991 or 1992, this is what I said about what the relationship meant for me:

> Since we came back [from Ireland], we've been reflecting on what those years meant, what mission is all about, what was most important about our time there. Recently we discovered a theme that helps us put it all together, that throws light on our experience: Mission as Hospitality—we go out as guests to another culture, they receive us as hosts, in any mission endeavor, and in the relationships that develop we exchange gifts, exchange blessings.[19]...
>
> God invites us into mission, into sharing with strangers, so that we can mutually bless each other, change each other, convert each other, and in the process both grow closer to the God who welcomes us in Jesus. This has been our experience. The longer we were in Ireland, the more we realized that what was happening was a two-way street.... "For I am longing to see you so that I may share with you some spiritual gift to strengthen you—or rather so that we may be mutually encouraged by each others' faith, both yours and mine," Paul writes in Romans 1:11-12....
>
> We went to Ireland convinced that our Mennonite way of being the church was something Ireland needed to see. ... But the longer we were there, the more we began to appreciate the faith of those people we went to serve—their long Christian tradition going back to the fourth century when St. Patrick started the Irish church;

their continued struggle to be faithful amid very demor-
alizing violence; their problems with unemployment[20]
and poverty. Here was a poor, economically depressed
country, yet when they saw starvation in Ethiopia, for
example, they gave more generously than any other
country. We found ourselves struggling alongside the
many peace groups in the country for some kind of reconciliation in Ireland and being impressed by how they
continued to fight against those forces that threatened to
overwhelm them.

Yes, we served them, but what we weren't expecting
was how much we gained, how much we would learn
from Irish Christians. Our experience of being guests in
the Irish culture encouraged our faith, enriched our
faith, to such an extent that I often feel I wasn't so much
called as sent to Ireland, by God, to learn from the Irish
culture, Irish people, Irish faith. My own life has been so
much enriched, blessed, changed, by the welcome I received there. That is part of God's purpose in drawing
us into mission—the mutual exchange of gifts that takes
place when we join our lives to others who are in some
sense "foreign" or "strange" to us.

We go out in mission to bring God, but we also go out
to find God, and we meet God, in unexpected places
and in unexpected ways, in the 'stranger.'"

So you can see that my Irish mission experience in a significant sense was a pilgrimage.[21] It formed me in indelible ways—
opening me and broadening me and, in the end, bringing me
back to my own tradition with a richer sense of its place and its
role in God's economy, in God's worldwide mission.[22]

Chapter Four

A WAKE-UP CALL!

Now we reach more fully the thesis—the purpose statement—of the project I did for my ministry degree. The
wording below is indebted to what I said then.

I think Mennonites have a problem. Many are not recognizing that we have a new spiritual situation: The communities
many of our forebears, and often we ourselves grew up in, no
longer exist in the same way. The spiritually formative environ-
ments—the largely Mennonite communities, the farms, the vil-
lages of southeastern, central, and western Pennsylvania; of
Ohio; of Iowa; of Virginia; of various other locales—have faded.
There is a lack of recognition that Mennonites today who are
younger than fifty or who have been grafted in through mission
outreach efforts have been formed much more by the American
culture or by ethnic subcultures within or beyond American society and sometimes by the other religious denominations
around them.

This adds richness but is very different from the way Mennonites were formed in the nineteenth and early twentieth centuries, as we have seen in my grandmother's life. Even though
some of these "Mennonite" farm communities still exist physi-
cally, the reality within which people live has changed—this reality is more influenced by popular culture, new roles for
women, world travel, the Internet, jobs, and higher education
within mainstream culture.

Conrad Kanagy's 2007 study, *Road Signs for the Journey: A
Profile of Mennonite Church USA*, includes statistics showing
that there are fewer Mennonite farmers today. "While 42 per-

cent of members report growing up on a farm, only 12 percent live on a farm today. This is a decline from 34 percent in 1972 to 25 percent in 1989 to 12 percent today."[1] Many are aware that Mennonites are no longer primarily farmers. What we don't realize fully, however, is that over 40 percent of our members in 2007 were people raised on a farm! They were spiritually formed in the environment I described in my grandmother's life story.

In twenty years, there will be few such members left. I am not lamenting this fact—I am just pointing out that these are nearly half our current members. We have counted on them and their almost-unconscious formation to help shape our identity. That will soon not be possible.

It's true that some North American Mennonites do recognize a new spiritual *kairos* moment or opportunity. (I am primarily describing members of the Mennonite Church USA.) Some have begun to do important rethinking; they have recognized a changing historical situation and considered how to promote spiritual growth in the twenty-first century. From my observation, parochial high school and college teachers are often most in touch with this reality and need. They know that the way they and many—if not most—American Mennonites were spiritually formed for the past 300 years is gone, leaving a vacuum that commercialism and other life patterns and influences have rushed in to fill.

In many ways, I am presenting a wake-up call. Hey, folks, we're living in a different world; we have different Christian formation needs! When I returned from Ireland in 1991 after twelve years away as a missionary, I was shocked at how Mennonites were often no longer visibly a *people* or subculture— with visibly different values and different attachments from those around them.

In becoming more like others outwardly, Mennonites are not alone. This is also true, in part, of other Christian groups traditionally more *separate*. As I talk about these ideas to other groups such as Quakers and read writings of Catholics, I hear them saying similar things: We have dropped our simple clothing and our simple speech patterns, say the Quakers, our Thees and Thous. New Quakers who are not "birthright" Quakers (their term for non-ethnic Quakers) need to be taught what silent meeting is all about, rather than learning it by osmosis from childhood on up.[2]

And Catholics, for instance New Testament scholar Sandra Schneiders, talk about changes that "vowed religious" (monks and nuns) went through after Vatican II. The new thinking of Vatican II moved them out of cloistered housing into small communities in ordinary neighborhoods and had them dressing more like other people, dropping their "habits" the way Mennonites dropped their "plain clothes." No longer living separated lives, they too, in many ways,92 went through a communal Dark Night of stripping off the way they formerly knew themselves.[3]

I find these commonalities fascinating and wonder if we can start sharing more with each other as denominations about how to live a Christian life in this century in the American culture. Since I know my own tradition best, I have chosen to join such a conversation by describing that tradition. Among those who have recognized the problem, I think there has been a necessary shift in understandings and practices of spiritual formation in the past thirty years. And we all could learn from each other.

I believe this shift could be described as a shift from an implicit to an explicit spirituality—one that can be explained to newcomers. It's a shift from a primarily communal spirituality to a spirituality that includes the personal. In the religious sociologist Robert Wuthnow's terms, it is a shift from a spirituality of "dwelling" to a spirituality of "seeking",[4] from a spirituality of "place" to a spirituality of "pilgrimage." Mennonite sociologist Delbert Wiens calls it a shift from a "village" spirituality to a "city" spirituality. I believe it is also a shift from a spirituality of separation from the world to a spirituality of separation from evil amid the world; from a spirituality focused on martyrdom to a spirituality of more hopeful participation in the world. And I think calling attention to this shift is a wake-up call.

Mennonites no longer live in those old spiritually formative structures; we are thus having to think about and choose spiritual practices. Some new *forms* need to be added to the Mennonite spiritual formation tool kit but with some distinctly

Mennonite sensibilities and themes. This shift is basically from a spiritual-formation-by-just-living-in-community to a more intentional spiritual-formation-by-contemplative-and-communal-disciplines.[5]

I described the spiritual formation practices of early twentieth-century Mennonites in the story of my grandmother, showing how Mennonites such as she carried the faith in every day, ordinary ways. But in my own story of formation we can see that these ways have become problematic or disappeared. However, I believe these practices and themes can be preserved and adapted to spiritually form contemporary Mennonites. One example of this preservation and adaptation has been the spiritual formation curriculum developed at Associated Mennonite Biblical Seminary (Elkhart, Ind.) since 1982. I'll look at this story in more depth in a subsequent chapter.

As stated earlier, this growth in the image of Christ used to happen primarily in cohesive geographical Mennonite communities, where formation happened implicitly rather than explicitly. An article in the *Mennonite Encyclopedia* by Marcus Smucker says that "Mennonite spirituality has been embedded in an ethical and communal way of life more than in self-conscious practices of piety such as meditation, fasting, contemplation. . . . [however] the experience of Christian community . . . has been diminishing among Western Mennonites."[6]

Dennis Martin says in the same encyclopedia that "The most significant trend in Mennonite spirituality in the late twentieth c. results from the disintegration of traditional Mennonite subcultures in Russia, Europe, and North America."[7] Martin then describes how in these subcultures "Mennonite spirituality was routinized and embedded in the patterns of life within the Mennonite communities. Worship followed regular patterns that were in effect liturgies; children were born into the community and 'grew into' the church" according to prescribed patterns or practices.

However, Martin observes,

As Mennonites left their subcultures or were forced to leave them by external pressures, the traditional . . . practices disappeared. Since there was no articulated and "portable" theology of liturgy or tradition that could be carried from the dissolving subculture into the new mainstream culture, a broad range of practices and theories filled the vacuum.[8]

We are becoming aware that we need to define more portable spiritual formation processes, now that our North American Mennonite geographical communities, the carriers of the tradition, are dissolving. When the people of Israel were exiled to Babylon, away from their sacred places and sacred land, the Torah and synagogue (both portable), became more crucial factors in their religious experience. Currently, Robert Wuthnow, observer of American spirituality, wonders whether the

> lived spirituality of many people in their private experi-
> ences of every day life may have changed over the
> course of the past half century. . . . [Is there] a shift from
> spirituality that is grounded decisively in an experience
> of place to one that is more aptly described as a spiritu-
> ality of seeking, negotiation, process?[9]

A more portable spiritual formation is necessary. But have Mennonites fully realized the vacuum Dennis Martin refers to, the vacuum that is there in our planning for spiritual formation?

Another of my concerns, another reason I interviewed my grandmother, is that there are potent themes and practices Mennonites have used more traditionally in spiritual formation, for example a practical, communal, plain and simple, ethical ethos, that should not be lost in our enthusiasm for new spiritual formation tools. Can Mennonites do spiritual formation in such a way as to minimize a total disconnect from this plain ethos, from what has gone before yet still sustain Anabaptists in a postmodern world?

I am also hoping that Mennonite spirituality begins to develop a more personal emphasis. My seminary training before 1980 (and I realize this is getting dated now) was overwhelmingly about the human will, about ethics, and about communal practices. It slighted other, more inward, personal and contemplative dimensions of human experience. The individual's inner life tended to be neglected. A contemporary Anabaptist psychologist, Allen Dueck, asks, "Do we really think we have metaphors for the inner life rich enough to nurture a radical discipleship in the present century? . . . An ethic without a rich inner piety generates cynicism, moralism, intellectualism, and hypocrisy."[10]

The Mennonite stress on ethics without equal attention to piety, I believe, already has generated cynicism and hypocrisy. A Mennonite spiritual growth process dare not disconnect inner and outer piety.

After my next chapter on definitions of words that we aren't familiar with, I want to look at the beginnings of the spiritual formation program in the 1980s at the Associated Mennonite Biblical Seminary. This program points to the future—to the need for new, more explicit means of spiritual formation, yet a faithful adaptation of the tradition my grandmother lived. This is a comprehensive Mennonite spiritual formation training program,[11] and it is time to reflect on this program's beginnings decades ago. I want to look at the directions this program points toward the future of the Mennonite church as a whole.

Finally, this book is an attempt to understand the various influences on my life, to understand why I journeyed toward contemplative spirituality, why that makes sense, why I'm not (I hope) crazy. I hope it will also help others by giving some language and some images to their search.

I am pointing to the need for new forms that can carry the values and themes that were important in my grandmother's life and can also address some of the gaps that were there. The shapes we live among shape *us*. Now that the shape of our lives is basically Western American, which in many ways is inimical to the Spirit (violence is the solution rather than love of enemies, time is a commodity to be bought, greed fuels much of our economy, our lives are fragmented, we are alienated from nature, we are addicted to busyness and stimulation) we need to be very intentional about giving a God-shape to our lives. Mennonite formation is necessarily changing from a formation-by-just-living-in-community to a more intentional spiritual formation-by-contemplative-and-communal-disciplines or practices.

Chapter Five

SOME NEW WORDS, SOME OLD

*S piritual formation, spiritual growth, spiritual disciplines, spiri-
tual direction, spirituality itself*—all need definition. These are
new words in Mennonite vocabulary, indeed in many non-
Catholic traditions, because they often come out of Catholic
monastic life. But Mennonites have done some work on definitions that I have found very helpful, particularly in the *Confession of Faith in a Mennonite Perspective* (1995). In this Confession
spiritual growth is defined in this way: "As we experience relationship with God, the life, death, and resurrection of Jesus
Christ take shape in us, and we grow in the image of Christ."[1]

This definition is so intriguing to me, but I haven't heard
much discussion or interest about what it might mean in any of
the circles I work within. What does it mean that "the life, death
and resurrection of Jesus Christ take shape within us?" What
does that look like? Is it reflected only in outward behavior?
How does it come about? I'd love to hear more discussion of
these questions: How does the life of Jesus take shape within
us? How does the death of Jesus take shape within us? How
does the resurrection of Jesus take shape within us?

Even the question of what it means to be spiritual is something that needs to be explored. My non-Mennonite theology
professor/adviser for my D.Min. thesis suggested I find a definition widely accepted in many Christian traditions. He suggested Urban T. Holmes III—an Episcopalian former dean of a
seminary who died in 1981. Holmes wrote a comprehensive—

evidently well-known—history of Christian spirituality that I wasn't familiar with.[2] Holmes says that "to be spiritual means. . . . that we are called to know God";[3] he sees us as "'unfinished' humans until we consent to . . . [the] power of the Spirit and are drawn into a wholeness of being." Holmes observes that "All the spiritual masters say that [spirituality] involves a relationship between God and humanity that we call prayer."[4]

Holmes' definition moves from knowing God, through opening to the Spirit, to prayer. His discussion of prayer then suggests some interesting movements, in that "authentic prayer requires us to move from familiar structure(s) to anti-structures . . . [T]he wilderness or desert experience—translatable into such devotional practices as silent retreats, pilgrimages, times alone, etc.—have a central place in the life of the Christian."[5] Later I will look at exactly these kinds of practices.

We need to define *spirituality* because the word, even the language of the spiritual, is new for some American Mennonites in this era. The *Mennonite Encyclopedia* of 1955 had no entries under the word *spiritual* except for "Spiritualism," an Anabaptist aberrant movement.[6] Mennonites had to work for years to be separated from "spiritualism" in church history definitions because of a movement at Münster (1500s Westphalia, Germany) that involved violence and sexual promiscuity. In fact, as early as Menno Simons, distinguishing Mennonites from "Spiritualists" was central to their ongoing self-definition. So there are reasons why the Spirit has been suspect in American Mennonite history.

But it's time to reinstate it. What do I mean by spirituality? To me, the word is synonymous with lived faith. When an Irish priest asked me in 1987 to describe Mennonite spirituality, I assumed he meant, What are the particular parameters of your lived faith? What is the peculiarly Mennonite charism (gift) or shape of faith? He didn't want to move me out of my basic spiritual mode, which a good spiritual director is always careful not to do. The same has been true as I work with a Quaker spiritual director. Her first attempt is to hear the shape of my own faith, and to build on that, then see where and how God might be inviting me to deeper faith within those parameters.

Kent Groff has a very interesting discussion of the word *spirituality* in a pamphlet from Oasis Ministries for Spiritual Development, Inc. Author of many books and founder of this Oasis organization, which trains spiritual directors in eastern and central Pennsylvania, Groff says we need a new English word because spirituality now means everything and anything.

You won't find it in the dictionary yet, but we need a new English word. Spirituality is becoming so subjective, fuzzy around the edges. When a person speaks of "my spirituality," it sounds so private, like something you put in your pocket. Today anything goes from thousand-dollar seminars with hot tubs to warmed up self-help psychology. Spirituality can refer to four-spiritual-laws kind of fundamentalism to abusive cults to narcissism without community. Today's spirituality has all the potential dangers and irrelevancies of yesterday's musty piety—and often lacks the critical thinking of sound theology.

At the same time, Groff believes that

theology can be so heavy on critical understanding that it loses its grounding in experiencing *faith in action* [my italics]. . . . One good way to convey that life in God is grounded in the life of the world is to avoid using the term "spirituality" alone. Speak of spiritual life, spiritual formation, or spiritual practices: place the emphasis on Spirit *and* human interaction. . . . Can we find one word that integrates *theology* and *ethics* with living faith? I propose *theopractice*.[7]

There are ongoing efforts to define spirituality. A 2006 book by David Augsburger, professor of pastoral care at Fuller Seminary, is called *Dissident Discipleship: A Spirituality of Self-Surrender, Love of God, and Love of Neighbor*. Augsburger has a helpful distinction between three forms of spirituality: the first focused around only one pole (self and discovery of depths of the self; Self as God), the second type oriented around two poles (self and God encounter), and the last, most Anabaptist and biblical spirituality, according to Augsburger, characterized by three poles (self-God-neighbor).[8] I have found this tripolar spirituality to be a helpful description of what Mennonite spirituality can be. The problem is that a tripolar spirituality focused on the neighbor sometimes tends to lose track of God, in my experience, and worship becomes a purely social experience—we share our concerns *with each other* and forget to also bring them to God to carry, for example.

The term *spiritual formation* needs to be defined as well. In interviews with Marlene Kropf and Marcus Smucker I discovered that, in the Mennonite tradition, *discipleship* is the more common word to denote our spirituality and spiritual formation. Following Jesus shapes us. Another important phrase Mennonites have used is *walking in the resurrection*.[9] But often the way Mennonites have trained people for discipleship or walking in the resurrection has not intentionally included all the necessary aspects of spiritual formation, such as prayer, reliance on the spirit, inner transformation, all of which are valued in the tradition if one looks hard enough. To continue to use these terms *discipleship* and *walking in the resurrection* requires some new content.

Perhaps *spiritual growth* is the more readily understandable term for Mennonites. Yet the term *formation* has an element that *spiritual growth* does not have—that of intentionally talking about *how* spiritual growth happens and paying attention to and directing the process of growth of another person or of a community. To ask the spiritual formation question is to ask, *How* does the life, death and resurrection of Jesus take shape in us? *How* do we grow in the image of Christ?

In "A Proposal for Spiritual Disciplines at AMBS," Marcus Smucker says that "Spiritual Formation is concerned with the particular means (practices, disciplines) by which our relationship with God, other, and self can be nurtured, the means for spiritual enrichment."[10] The "means," the "how," are crucial. He then goes on to root this concern for the how of formation in the biblical story.

> Spiritual formation is concerned with a variety of contemplative disciplines by which we open ourselves to God so that we grow in love for God, and are trans-

formed into the likeness of God (2 Cor. 3:18). Even as Jesus was "made perfect" (Heb. 5:9) through his encounters with God (John 5: 16-30) we too are being "changed" (*metamorphometha*) into God's likeness from one degree of glory to another (2 Cor. 3:18) as we abide in him.[11]

In the 1990 edition of *Mennonite Encyclopedia*, volume 5, Smucker says,

> Although the terms *spiritual formation* and *spiritual direction* initially came from the Eastern Orthodox and Roman Catholic contemplative traditions, these concepts are clearly taught in the Scriptures. Christians are to have the mind of Jesus who was in the form (*morphe*) of God, but also took on the form of a servant in our behalf (Phil. 2:6-7). . . . The biblical pattern is for Jesus to be formed in believers, as he was in the form of God. . . . Although, until recently, Mennonites did not use the terms *spiritual formation* and *spiritual direction* to describe their religious experience, concern for formation and direction have been inherent in Mennonite emphasis upon discipleship. Anabaptist and Mennonite discipleship has been a spirituality shaped by the ethical imperative to follow Jesus at all costs.[12]

Smucker mentions the many examples of formation in the Scriptures: Paul's statement of longing to the church in Galatia that Christ would be formed in them (Gal. 4:19), the transforma*tion* that takes place by the renewing of our minds (Rom. 12: 2, my italics). Although Mennonites have not traditionally used the term *spiritual formation*, the examples of *being formed into Christ* in the Scriptures are there.

Formation could also be called "shaping"—how the shape of our lives also shapes us. Formation was originally a Catholic term to describe the process by which novices in a religious order became full-fledged members or monks. Mennonites do not consciously have a process like this, although the process of membership classes before baptism and then subsequently, "growing in faith," has some elements of this. However, as mentioned in the beginning, the way this formation or growth used to happen in the past, was by simply being a daily part of a "shaping" community .

I am increasingly intrigued by the realization that formation is not a word that originated in the Protestant or Mennonite traditions. I believe it is a word—as I say above—that was coined and defined originally by Catholic religious orders to describe their ways of incorporating new monks or nuns into their particular religious orders such as the Franciscan or Benedictine orders. I asked a Benedictine sister what formation meant for her and she said it was about teaching the new sisters the history and particular identity of the order they were joining. I said, "So formation is about the information you teach them?" and she said, "Well, formation is also about living with the community."

The implications of her answer for us are worth thinking about.

I wonder if formation is a word Catholics would use to talk about how ordinary Catholic lay people are formed in the faith. I don't think so. We need to be aware that we are taking a term and redefining it.

Another key word for me is *practices*. The concept of *practice* has been clarified by philosopher Alisdair MacIntyre, who draws ultimately on Aristotle. MacIntyre defines practice as "any coherent form of socially established cooperative human activity."[13] Wuthnow and others have subsequently used practice to define a new approach to spirituality, which is "practice-based."[14] Another example is in the book *Practicing Our Faith*, where editor Dorothy Bass describes "Christian" practices as a way of living well in our modern era. "These are ordinary activities, the stuff of everyday life. Yet all of them, no matter how mundane, can be shaped in response to God's active presence. And all of them, woven together, suggest the patterns of a faithful Christian way of life for our time."[15]

"Practices" are "patterns" which "shape" us. An enormous topic! What practices do we practice? And how do they shape us? I will come back to this at the end.

The word *contemplation* or *contemplative prayer* is almost as nebulous as "spirituality." I have had a hard time understanding what it means, but that is partly, I understand now, because it is something that needs to be experienced before one can understand the definition. It is also because contemplation is a very unfamiliar word or practice to most Protestants. The Catholic tradition has held the practice of contemplative prayer until very recently. Here is the definition that comes closest to my own experience. It is from a book by Catholic scholar and nun, Sandra Schneiders, called *New Wineskins*.

> Contemplative prayer differs in important ways from the kind of prayer we can engage in by our own efforts of thinking and willing. Contemplation is freely given by God. We cannot bring it about no matter what we do. Precisely for this reason it fills the one receiving it with a profound conviction of the reality and presence of God. It is an affectively involving, psychologically transforming experience of the presence and activity of God in the very depths of one's being. In its joyful moments it is an experience of being marvelously and intimately touched, loved, cherished—and enabled to respond from depths one does not control, did not even know one possessed.[16]

Contemplation is very simply looking at or being in the presence of something or someone with eyes that go deeper, ears that are more attuned to the sounds around—a slowed down gazing or hearing—of what is present to us. It is attentiveness, very simply, to "what is." We experience it every day when we stop to look at the clouds even for a moment, or slow down to really pay attention to another person. These are some of the everyday experiences of contemplation that contemplative or "listening prayer" builds on. Think of Elijah and the still small voice—the voice that was not in the earthquake or in the fire or in anything that came and bowled him over. Think of Moses slowing down to notice the burning bush and going over to get a better look at it. If Moses had not gone over, would he have received his call from God to set his people free? There are invitations all around us all the time.

Indeed, one might say that in contemplation is the way forward for our cultural ills—the way forward as the church addresses Western culture's focus on control and dominance (suggested in an article by Carmelite nun from Baltimore Constance FitzGerald).[17]

Occasionally I will refer to *spiritual direction*—a one-to-one meeting between two people, [18] in which one person serves as director and the other as directee, listening together for God's presence in the directee's life. The classic work on spiritual direction was written in 1982 by two Catholic priests, William Barry and William Connolly.[19] Following their definition, "spiritual direction is concerned with helping a person directly with his or her relationship with God . . . [asking] 'Who is God for me, and who am I for [God]?'"[20] They see

> Christian spiritual direction . . . as help given by one Christian to another which enables that person to pay attention to God's personal communication to him or her, to respond to this personally communicating God, to grow in intimacy with this God, and to live out the consequences of the relationship. The focus of this type of spiritual direction is on experience, not ideas.[21]

Usually spiritual direction is most effective if it is done by a person trained by other spiritual directors and by one who is also a recipient of spiritual direction.

Finally, I have used a German word—Gelassenheit—in looking at what shaped my grandmother, and it will become even more important in my last chapter. Walter Klaassen says that this was a concept borrowed from medieval mystics, by sixteenth-century South German and Austrian Anabaptists.[22] A scholar named Robert Friedmann, according to Klaassen, "first reacquainted Mennonites with the mystic concept. He found it in the writings of South German and Austrian Anabaptists and discovered that it described a crucial part of [these Anabaptists'] concept of the Christian life, especially their relationship to God."

In the *Mennonite Encyclopedia* Friedmann defines Gelassenheit as "self-surrender, resignation in God's will, yieldedness to God's will, self-abandonment, the (passive) opening to God's willing, including the readiness to suffer for the sake of God, also peace and calmness of mind, in Dutch devotional literature."[23] What strikes me is that the term has continued to be used through all four centuries of the Anabaptist-Mennonite tradition, through the present, and might therefore be fruitful and central in the future.

I presuppose that the Mennonite situation in today's world is not totally distinct from the general society's. A statement by non-Mennonite Tilden Edwards applies to Mennonites as much as it does to other modern people. He says there are millions of people in our society who "seek an ongoing 'soul-awareness.'" He believes that "Religious professionals" are not always able to respond to this seeking because they have "a theological/philosophical preparation that deals with human beings largely in broad abstractions. Missing is *an adequate bridge that can link the depth of historical . . . religious experience . . . concretely with a person's unique situation*" (my italics).[24] One-to-one spiritual direction provides that bridge. This is what I believe Mennonites also need to work on. A one-size-fits-all spiritual guidance that only comes via the pulpit to the congregation or crowd is not enough. Individual Christians also need help to discern how their particular life story fits within the larger God-story, in very concrete terms, in detail, to make their faith meaningful in their particular daily life, the life that God is incarnate in.

I believe that when people lose a religious subculture, they experience (as a whole people), a Dark Night of the Soul. In a Dark Night, God is experienced more as hidden. In turn, the need is to experience God more directly, without intermediary, through silence and other contemplative practices (apophatic spirituality), rather than primarily through cultural practices (kataphatic spirituality).[25] This might explain why the interest in apophatic spirituality and apophatic practices like solitude and silence has exploded among Mennonites.

I hypothesize that Mennonites are experiencing a stripping away of their previous experience of God, a loss of their customary communal/agricultural forms of knowing God, and are searching for new patterns and practices.[26] I was shocked and astounded to find a book by Catholic scholar Sandra Schneiders after I finished writing my thesis that also uses this Dark Night concept to describe what religious orders of monks and nuns went through after they "lost" some of their previous practices following the changes of Vatican II.[27] Not just monks and nuns but ordinary Catholics experienced a great wrenching when the Mass was changed from Latin to the vernacular of each country. I was struck with the similarities to those of my ancestors experiencing the change from German to English in the 1930s in my local area.

The *Confession of Faith in a Mennonite Perspective* statement on spirituality stresses equally the two parts of the Great Commandment: loving God (piety) and loving neighbor (social relationships/social holiness). The confession says: "Anabaptists and Mennonites . . . do not separate spirituality from ethics, or reflection from action. For this reason, this confession of faith includes spirituality in the section on discipleship."[28] "We believe that to be a disciple of Jesus is to know life in the Spirit. As we experience relationship with God, the life, death, and resurrection of Jesus Christ take shape within us."[29]

Early Anabaptist Hans Denck (1495-1527) said it well, "No one can truly know [Christ] unless [one] follows him in life."[30] What is not so widely quoted by Mennonites, but which is also a theological foundation for this book is Denck's next line, that "no one may follow Christ unless [one] has first known him."[31] Ethics and spirituality—discipleship rooted in a deep knowing—we need to keep these together.

The biblical rationale for Mennonites to stress the Christian's deeply personal communion with God is the paradigm of Jesus' life. Jesus had a relationship of intimacy with his Father whom he called "Abba," which sustained him at his baptism, through his life's work of teaching and healing, and to which he withdrew regularly in prayer, particularly as he faced decisions about his mission and as he faced the cross. We, as Christ's followers, are invited to and need the same. The Gospel of John passage of the Vine and branches is instructive: "We draw the life of the Spirit from Jesus Christ, just as a branch draws life from the vine. Severed from the vine, the power of the Spirit cannot fill us. But as we make our home in Christ and Christ abides in us, we bear fruit and become his disciples."[32]

Looking to the paradigm of Jesus—and his relationship to his father—is a strategy that we as Mennonites find authoritative; it packs a lot of clout for us. In an interview, Marcus Smucker said,

For me, the two [a relationship of intimacy with God and social-ethical/peace concerns] belong together. Theologically they belong together. . . . [In] the great commandment: "Love the Lord your God with all your heart, mind and soul, and your neighbor as yourself" . . . you have the two sides of the thing [the two sides] of this equation."

Mennonites talk about following Jesus and discipleship is following Jesus, Smucker says:

In the passages in John 5 and John 14, we have a very personal language about Jesus with the Father. This is something we don't hear in Mennonite circles in relation to discipleship, but it belongs [biblically]. . . . The two go together—the deeply personal and the profoundly communal. If you only have the personal and not the communal elements, with the necessary accountability, you end up with a personalized, truncated gospel. But if you have only the communal commitment without a deeply personal relationship with God, you lose the vitality and gospel power needed to truly follow Jesus in all of life.[33]

If any one sentence would summarize my core concerns in this book, it would be Smucker's last one here. If we have only the communal element of our faith, we lose the "vitality and power needed to truly follow Jesus in all of life." We also need a deeply personal relationship with God such as the one modeled in Jesus' life. Following Jesus involves participating in that same relationship with "Abba," not just participating in the cross. Following Jesus is about participating in God, in the Spirit, in the fellowship of the Three-in-One.

There are precedents for Smucker's claim in earlier Anabaptist theology. Mennonite college professor and historian John Roth describes an increasing recognition on the part of Mennonite scholars that "the language of grace, the call for personal piety, the inner experience of the believer are an organic necessary part of the Anabaptist/ Mennonite tradition, not some sort of alien influence."[34]

Chapter Six

NEW SPIRITUAL DIRECTIONS FOR A SEMINARY

In my research for my thesis, besides looking at my grandmother's life, I also wanted to know why a spiritual formation curriculum was implemented at the seminary where I studied. This program began sometime after I graduated in 1979, and I wanted to know exactly when it started, why it started, and what its content was, so I began to do research on this at the same time as I researched the story of my grandmother. The thesis then attempted to link these two research projects—comparing and contrasting or at least putting them side-by-side to see what could be learned.

From 1974-1979, I attended a Mennonite seminary in Indiana, now Associated Mennonite Biblical Seminary, as a young twenty-something. (My story seems to be moving backward in time.) Later, in the 1980s while I was in Ireland, I began to hear about a program of spiritual formation starting there. I was fascinated for many reasons—one was because I believe this program points a way forward for the whole church in terms of our spiritual formation task.

I focus on four of the people who I discovered were instrumental in the beginnings of that program, though many others at the seminary, for instance Erland Waltner, laid the groundwork and carried a concern for spiritual growth. These four are

Thelma Groff, Marcus Smucker, Marlene Kropf, and Marlin Miller.

I especially became intrigued with the similarities in their stories—they were all involved in either overseas mission or inner-city ministry and thus were separated from the traditional structures of American Mennonite community for a time, as I was. As a result of these experiences, they were all drawn toward a more intentional focus on "spirituality" or "spiritual formation."[1]

These four people, meeting eventually as staff at AMBS, recognized a need in the 1970s and 1980s for new approaches to spiritual formation, particularly for training pastors. This need was also reflected in the wider church at the time. Concerns to deepen spiritual life or piety among Mennonites date back at least to the 1970s. One example is Gene and Mary Herr,[2] a Mennonite couple who started what they called "discipleship" units. These were households of Mennonite youth doing some kind of voluntary service work, often in inner cities, combined with intentional leadership to promote the youths' personal spiritual growth. Jim Lapp, former Conference Pastor of Franconia Mennonite Conference, mentioned to me that these discipleship units were essentially spiritual formation units, started in the 1970s with spiritual formation agenda.[3]

I found out that in 1978 this same Mary Herr was also commissioned by the Mennonite Women's Missionary and Service Commission to conduct silent retreats throughout North America with Mennonite women's groups. A women's group was selected in each area conference and Mary traveled to these places and led silent retreats where she taught contemplative prayer practices.[4]

One of these retreats was deeply formative for Marlene Kropf, a Mennonite high school teacher in Oregon, who eventually became associate professor at AMBS and is now also Minister of Worship for Mennonite Church USA.

Other examples include the many Mennonites who began seeing Catholic spiritual directors, going to monasteries, or attending Catholic worship services in the 1970s. (Catholics were the ones who carried the contemplative tradition at that point in history; there were not as many Protestant resources.) I am aware especially of people in the Elkhart, Indiana, area who began taking courses at Notre Dame and attending Catholic masses there during the 1970s when I lived there. But I would like to focus particularly on what happened at the Mennonite seminary in Elkhart, since I attended there. In learning more about how the spiritual formation program started, and what the content of that program was, I thought I could answer my question: "What is the shape of Mennonite spiritual formation?"

Courses in Mennonite spiritual formation also began at Eastern Mennonite Seminary in Harrisonburg, Virginia, which would bear investigation. I have had correspondence about that program with two key professors there, John Martin and Wendy Miller, and if I had time I would love to research its beginnings further. But I couldn't research two seminaries and my grandmother's story, and also get a thesis done. Someone else will have to research EMS.

In the 1970s when I was at Goshen Biblical Seminary,[5] spirituality courses were nonexistent, the word itself relatively unknown even in the broader society. The three courses which addressed concerns of the God-human relationship were "Devotional Life" taught by J. C. Wenger, and "Discipleship" and "God" taught by Clarence Bauman. I was intrigued by Clarence Bauman, and I took at least one of his classes, but I also at the time (possibly unfairly) viewed him as a little on the fringe or extreme. However, his classes on "God" and "Discipleship" introduced me to the idea that there were more "mystical" branches of the Anabaptist tree. Clarence Bauman, I later discovered, also led silent meetings at the seminary in those days and was known to have a retreat cottage to which he retired periodically.

There was a warm personal faith expressed by certain professors. In Millard Lind's Old Testament classes, for example, I remember him praying before class in such a way that the class understood that his concern with the Old Testament was not purely academic but also reflected his own passion for God and God's work in the world throughout history.

However, I think it would be fair to say that in many classes there was a general sense of suspicion about "spiritualizing" the Bible or biblical texts. By that I understood taking the meat out of the ethical imperatives by spiritualizing the stories and teachings, which is what other faith traditions did, according to my professors. We were concerned in those early days of discovering *The Politics of Jesus* (published 1972)[6] not to de-historicize, depoliticize, "spiritualize" the ministry of Jesus.

I heard often, in my studies, about the "vertical" dimension of faith as contrasted with the "horizontal" dimension. The vertical dimension was characterized as a "me and God" emphasis, while the horizontal dimension, stressed as more Mennonite, included accountability in the community of faith, the peace emphasis, the ethical content of Jesus' teachings. The emphasis in those years, at that place, was on the horizontal. However, for me it resulted in denigrating what was labeled the vertical—anything individual or personal or relationship-to-God-oriented. I came out of seminary suspicious of personal prayer, almost convinced that the only real prayer was communal.

Looking back, I see now that this unequal stress on the outward implications of faith, while an important corrective to other traditions, was a convenient way for Mennonite young people like myself to ignore inner personal issues and label that disinterest in the inner life "Anabaptist." I do remember thinking at the time that there must be a way of having a personal faith without having it be "individualistic" and purely "vertical" (the two bad words). But I'm not sure I would have said that in my circle of friends, many of whom were reading and studying with John Howard Yoder.[7]

However, as I moved on in life after seminary and began practicing "the politics of Jesus" in a peace ministry in Ireland, the "outer-ness" of a purely political gospel wore thin. I began to long for a life of prayer that could sustain me over the long haul in Ireland as I faced loneliness, the breakdown of our communal living arrangement, troubled relationships with fellow missionaries, violence in the inner city where we lived, and political violence in the rest of Ireland. As our intentional community broke down, I lost my access to God, because that access had been too purely communal.

That was when I began to hear inklings of a spiritual formation program beginning at the seminary. In my 1986 AMBS alumni bulletin, I heard about a new subject called "Mennonite spirituality." Since this focus coincided remarkably with my own journey to learn more about prayer, I developed an intense curiosity about what was going on there and why. In 1998, I entered the Doctor of Ministry program at Lancaster Theological Seminary with the desire to explore this subject.

In 2001 I started taking one of my electives for the D.Min. from Marcus Smucker, Professor Emeritus of Pastoral Theology from AMBS, who had recently moved to Lancaster. I remember clearly the first day of this elective class and the moment when I told him I was interested in how the spiritual formation program started at AMBS. He said, "Well, I started the program." Later he clarified that Thelma Groff[8] had also been part of the beginnings of the program.

Even more remarkable was that Marcus Smucker told me the program began largely as a result of the vision of Marlin Miller, then president of the seminary! Marlin was a mentor and well known to me as an intellectual person, a person of faith, but a person with whom I had never talked specifically about prayer or his personal walk with God. I had carpooled to the seminary with Marlin and others. My husband and I had been in Marlin's and his wife Ruthann's small group at the Assembly Church. Marlin had in fact brought the proposal for mission in Ireland to our attention, and one night in his living room he introduced us to Mike Garde. He was my teacher for several excellent seminary courses. He and Ruthann spent a half-year sabbatical with us in Ireland in 1985 or 1986, some of that time babysitting for us to relieve us of our parental duties. (Marlin also lectured on the gospel of peace and did other scholarly work while he was there.) I'd had no idea through those years of his concern for spirituality.

Tragically Marlin died of a heart attack in 1994, so by the time I got started on this research, I could not interview him. I have tried instead to reconstruct some of the history from interviews with Marcus Smucker and Marlene Kropf[9] and e-mail correspondence with others.

Marlin became president of Goshen Biblical Seminary in 1975 and later president of AMBS. Before that he had lived with Ruthann and family in Europe from 1963 to 1974.[10] He originally went to study for his doctorate at Heidelberg (graduated 1968) and afterward accepted an assignment with Mennonite Board of Missions (MBM) working with African students.[11] In 1974, he returned with Ruthann and family to his home area in Indiana, and was visiting professor at Goshen Biblical seminary from 1974-75, when I was a first-year student. He became president of GBS the following year and continued to teach theology. His career at AMBS lasted until his untimely death.[12]

Sometime between when he started teaching at the seminary in 1974 and 1982 when some spiritual disciplines classes began, Marlin must have seen a need for more focus on formation. He evidently began to see a way forward in the work Marcus Smucker, a Mennonite pastor, was doing in Oregon. A key part of the story is in the meeting of Miller with Smucker in the 1970s.

Similar to Marlin Miller's living in a major city in the 1960s and 1970s (in Miller's case, Heidelberg and Paris), Smucker was a pastor in an inner-city congregation in Portland, Oregon. During those years, Smucker also began rethinking faith. He struggled with his own spiritual journey and as a result began bringing some new spiritual formation agenda to the Portland Mennonite congregation.

Smucker and Miller met in the 1970s. During those years, Smucker, in addition to pastoring, was a member of the AMBS Seminary Board and became chair of the board from the mid-1970s until 1982. "While I was chair, when Marlin would occasionally come to Portland he found out what we were doing in spiritual formation and became very interested," Smucker said. "Marlin had a keen intellect, and he also had a significant piety. He seemed to sense that what I was doing in Portland [was something he wanted for the seminary]."[13]

What was Smucker doing in the congregation? I asked when I interviewed him. He gave me this explanation, with some personal background. In the mid-1970s, during his twelfth year as a pastor of the Portland Mennonite Church, Smucker took time off during the summer because he was experiencing deep burnout. "In those years I had been very active in ministry in the inner city as well as working with a congregation that was growing. I was just too involved in too many things."[14]

Smucker, as ex-Amish, inner-city pastor, tried several ways of renewing himself after the first twelve years. Some were more or less successful. Finally, after sixteen years of pastoral ministry, a friend told him of a silent retreat option.

> I took three days and two nights in the Mt. Hood forest by myself, for a time of fasting, praying, reflecting and journaling. This was a watershed experience for me spiritually. This was the first time I experienced prolonged solitude. From that experience, I began to realize there was a whole new way to nurture myself, spiritually and emotionally, that I hadn't known before. Almost simultaneously Marlene Kropf [member of my congregation at that time] did a contemplative weekend with Gene and Mary Herr. Soon after that we began leading spirituality retreats and also weekly contemplative groups in the congregation.[15]

So another key part of the story was the intersection of Marcus Smucker's and Marlene Kropf's interests and life experience in the Portland congregation in the 1970s. How did she become acquainted with spiritual formation tools and contemplative prayer? I asked her in a 2002 interview. She described to me in this interview[16] how she came back from an MCC term in Jamaica (1974-76), basically

> broken in many ways. . . . I had an intuition about this [before I left]. I wrote in my journal: "I don't know if my faith will survive for two years in a foreign country," because it's always been connected with the [Mennonite] community. And it nearly didn't. That's why I started on an intentional journey when I got back, because the violence [in Jamaica], the lack of nourishment in ways that I recognized and could receive, wore me down. And I found myself facing my own lack of a vital connection with God by the end of that two years.[17]

I noticed here especially the missionary experience— the physical separation from "place" and communal Mennonite structures—that prompted Kropf's interest in spirituality, or as she calls it here, a more vital connection to God.

These two life stories, Kropf's and Smucker's, and their combined teaching, leading, and nurturing of a vital spirituality in the Portland congregation, caught the attention of Marlin Miller. When Smucker left Oregon and moved to Indiana later to study and so his children could attend the local Mennonite high school, Miller soon invited him to come to the seminary to teach and give direction to a spiritual formation program for potential pastors.

Because President Miller died so young, it is not possible to ask him why he felt this was something he wanted for the seminary. But I reconstructed some of his thinking from an article called "A Genuine Biblical Spirituality"[18] he wrote in the denominational magazine in 1982, the year the spiritual formation program started at AMBS.

In the article Miller begins with a discussion about why an "emphasis on prayer, meditating on the Scriptures and the inner life is . . . needed in the church."[19] Interestingly, and perhaps as a result of his own mission experience, he first describes the results of a survey of missionaries about "problems they had in overseas work." He notes that missionaries listed as problems such things as pursuing a devotional life, having friends with whom to let down one's hair, doubts over their call, sexual temptations, a feeling of being useless or not properly appreciated, relations with other missionaries . . . " and then his uniquely dry sense of humor comes out in this statement: "The answer may have been partly predictable: after all, it is more 'spiritual' to admit having a problem in pursuing regular devotions than having squabbles with other missionaries."[20] Yet he comes back to the lack of regular attention to the inner life as key, and he goes on to say that if this is a problem for missionaries, it is also most likely a problem for "normal" congregational members. "'Normal' congregational members," he says,

> as well as missionaries can easily become so busy working, witnessing, and serving others—or simply in pursuing other interests—that they neglect their devotional life. Then spiritual fatigue sets in. Without the disci-

plines of praying, reading the Bible, and nurturing the inner life, Christians will hardly be able to avoid spiritual emptiness or even burn-out, let alone continue to grow in faith and spiritual maturity. Cultivating a genuine Christian spirituality will therefore include the disciplines of prayer, meditation on Scriptures, and opening the inner life to God.[21]

He then describes the upside-down kingdom and how our spirituality needs to be built on Jesus' concern for the underdog. Here is a clear statement of Miller's concern for the church and perhaps also his dream for the seminary. He concludes with a call for a "spirituality which expresses itself in *both* private prayer *and* public practice without playing one off against the other."[22]

"Private prayer and public practice without playing one off against the other." Perhaps this is what Miller saw happening in Portland, in the congregation where Smucker and Kropf were active in both spirituality in the congregation and ministry in the city. This is how Kropf thinks it happened:

I think that [when Marlin] came to the Portland congregation . . . and saw what Marcus was doing in the congregation . . . that . . . opened his eyes to what should be happening with pastoral formation . . . that's what needed to be embedded in pastoral training. And without Marlin's support, it would never have flown at AMBS at that point. . . . I think [Marlin's] interest came from his own "reading" of pastoral ministry. He was very much involved in the Leadership and Authority discussions [documents being prepared in the Mennonite church at that time].

"In fact," Kropf believes,

he wrote the church-wide document on leadership and authority, and my "reading" of it is that he sensed the spiritual bankruptcy of Mennonite pastors. He himself was a person of deep faith. He was a pious man, in the best sense of that word. He was a pious man who loved the church and wanted pastors to provide spiritual leadership. He came back to AMBS sort of at the tail-end of the activist and Barthian era, where there was suspicion of piety, . . . I think he saw what was missing. . . . I think it was [Marlin's] own personal faith, his own vision of what spiritual leadership means in the church, and . . . he was able to see what was missing because he'd been outside the North American environment for some time and he came back and saw it.[23]

Kropf's comments very much confirm that Marlin Miller was at the center of this beginning program. She notices that he had, in fact, come to this conclusion that Mennonite life was almost "bankrupt" spiritually [her own strong word] precisely because he had been separated from the Mennonite communal structures for over a decade.

In focusing on Miller, Smucker, and Kropf, I don't want to neglect others involved and supportive at that point. Certainly other faculty were aware of a need at the seminary. I wrote to several who were already at AMBS when the program began in 1982 and asked why the program began. Weyburn Groff, retired professor, pointed to ways that the spirituality emphasis began long before the 1980s.[24] C. J. Dyck, professor emeritus, had become aware of the importance of a spiritual life concentration during a year with the Benedictines, in Collegeville, Minnesota, in 1972-73, and he had been teaching a "Devotional Life" class at AMBS. However, he says he does not remember Marlin Miller talking in faculty meetings[25] about needing a spiritual-formation emphasis at the seminary.[26] Gayle Gerber Koontz, professor of theology and ethics, says that

> the program resulted in part from a felt-need on the part of faculty (while strong family/personal devotions and related piety characterized previous generations of Mennonite families and seminary students, this could not be assumed for students arriving in the late '70s) meeting the vocational call and analysis of the "spirituality" situation of the larger church which Marcus and later Marlene carried while at AMBS.[27]

Jake Elias, professor of New Testament, says the program in spiritual formation was largely a result of the recognition that even though we had had courses on "The Devotional Life" (J. C. Wenger) and "Discipleship" (Clarence Bauman), and even though we had thrice-weekly chapels, and encouragement toward regular prayer, we did not have a focused effort toward forming persons in the area of their relationship with God. Some of the initiative in the 1980s came out of Marcus Smucker's interests, but this also arose out of a felt need not only to shape people's minds and develop their skills but also to form their "souls" (their inner person, their relationship to God).[28]

And finally, I have discovered that Erland Waltner, professor emeritus and past president of the seminary, spoke in his inaugural address in 1958 "with deep yearning, of a vision that AMBS might be as much a place of prayer as a place of scholarship."[29] In his later life at the seminary, Waltner assisted Smucker in spiritual direction with students and continued to do so for some years.

Kropf also refers in her interview to the sense that a new generation of students coming through the seminary did not have a vital prayer life. She identifies some of the reasons for that, which can also be seen as reasons for the shift in spirituality in the church as a whole, noting that "after the breakdown of community . . . after the '40s and '50s with the [Mennonite] move to urban centers, with the rise of formal education, with the rise of affluence, Mennonites got unattached from their communal roots." Kropf believes that when "faith that was so much nurtured by the communal environment" was no longer receiving such support, now that Mennnonites "weren't there with those grandparents who prayed in ways that we knew God was real, then we lost our heart connection to God." She concludes that "the loss of community in my generation was the big loss.[30]

The loss of community was key because not having those people around you meant that you had to find your own way spiritually.

And so, when you don't have those people, and you have to find your way to God yourself, and you haven't

been taught the classical spiritual disciplines, [then
that's hard]. . . . It wasn't until that silent retreat with
Mary Herr in 1978 that I was taught a way to [read the
Bible and pray so] that I could actually hear something
from God![31]

The classical spiritual disciplines emerge here in Kropf's
narrative as crucial because they allow one more direct access
to God, through proven methods of listening prayer, through
silence. Kropf says no one had ever taught her before how to really hear God. (Notice the resemblances to Marcus Smucker's
first silent retreat, as revelatory of a new way to hear God.) The
contemplative classical disciplines make sense now, they are
not just arbitrary new forms of spiritual nurture, because they
promote more receptivity to God, more listening and less talking to God, in an age when we can't rely on others to always
hear God for us.

I remember the first large Mennonite gathering I attended
after returning from Ireland, when the convenor suggested that
we all pray in small groups. The noise that erupted was so loud,
as everyone began talking to God, that I wondered how God
was ever going to get a word in edgewise. Addressing such a
milieu with a new understanding of the need to listen to God
explains in part why the seminary chose the contemplative (listening prayer) forms they did for their spiritual formation curriculum.

Kropf goes on to explain how one can become spiritually
"bankrupt," even while being a part of church structures:

And I was all the while an active church member. It's
very possible to live on that heritage without having
one's own direct connection to God. . . . It's mediated
through the community. It's [mediated] through the
structures. . . . As long as you have the communal structures, you don't know that you're spiritually bankrupt. . . . You live off other people's connections to God
or the community's inheritance. But I think you spend
that inheritance in one generation.[32]

Here she seems to point strongly toward "having one's
own direct connection to God." I believe this is at the heart of

the shift that is taking pace in Mennonite spirituality. To have one's own direct connection to God was not a stated goal of Mennonite life when I was in seminary in the 1970s. And although it is a strong statement, I believe she is talking about her own experience in Jamaica, when she says that "as long as you have the communal structures, you don't know that you're spiritually bankrupt."

Even if we tone down the language and say "spiritually needy" instead of "bankrupt," I think Kropf's words here explain why there is much more interest in spirituality in some sectors of the Mennonite world than in others. Mennonites who still live primarily in the vestiges of the old agrarian communal structures do not feel as urgent a need to get a closer connection to God. Their connection is strong, I would contend. However, the holy is mediated more through "place" and through communal structures than through finding ways to "hear" God.[33]

These are some of the reasons the more intensive focus on spiritual formation began at the seminary. At the beginning, I learned it involved some hard work of integrating the spirituality agenda into the life of the seminary. Smucker described this two-year process to me in the interview.[34] In hindsight, he sees this process of faculty ownership as helpful theologically. It wasn't just about politics: "The fact that I had to develop that program in the presence of all the faculty meant that I was developing the program in [a] context that was thoroughly Anabaptist."[35]

He had to justify the program to people who taught history, theology, peace, the Bible, ethics. A spiritual formation program begun in the context of being accountable to all those disciplines would therefore have a uniquely Anabaptist flavor: concerned for communal, congregational life; committed to peacemaking; biblically based; and focused on the living out of Christian faith, i.e., on ethics. Indeed the program was formulated in conversation within the community of the seminary, the process itself reflecting a Mennonite communal bias.

Both Smucker and Kropf stress that even after the program started, they were constantly trying to work at the agenda of Anabaptist-Mennonite spirituality. Smucker says now that even as he was developing the program in spirituality at AMBS, I was constantly giving thought to, and reflecting with students about the intersection of the contemplative with Mennonite/ Anabaptist thought, asking, "How is this content and experience different than or similar to traditional Mennonite thought and experience?"[36]

Kropf sees a strength of the program as being "the intentional way we tried to be faithful to our Anabaptist tradition. I don't think we ever went into a class without consciously engaging in that interpretive process."[37] She observes that

> in fact, Marcus and I draw heavily from our childhood formation in the Mennonite church [in our teaching on spiritual formation. There was an] implicit [Mennonite spiritual formation in those childhood experiences]. . . . I can now point back to my childhood church experience in a Mennonite church in Oregon and Marcus often goes back to his Amish roots, and he knows and I know that we were certainly shaped by that and brought that sensibility to where we are. But the other piece that I think can't be ignored is that both of us were part of an urban Mennonite congregation in the '60s and '70s and '80s.[38]

This urban life experience seems to have shaped the spirituality that grew out of their Amish and Mennonite childhoods into a responsive, socially committed spirituality engaged in the world—a spirituality stressing outer social responsibility and inner personal renewal at the same time.

As the program in spiritual formation developed at AMBS, Smucker and his then co-worker Thelma Groff wrote a statement to the seminary board reflecting on their thoughts and experiences in the first year of offering spirituality and formation courses[39] and affirming that

> a Mennonite spirituality must be reflected in the life of the congregation and in the world as well as a personal experience. . . . Our experience in this community suggests one place to begin a conscious effort in spirituality is in the area of the personal. . . . One goal could be for each student to embrace certain disciplines or practices

for his/her personal spiritual growth while at AMBS. . . . We begin with the personal because we believe there is a need for such emphasis at AMBS at this time. In this community we have significant emphasis upon our corporate life and social concerns; we believe more attention must be given to personal spiritual development for a more balanced life in the Spirit.[40]

Many of our Mennonite churches still need to begin here—I believe there is still a need for a "more balanced life in the Spirit." Personal spirituality is what often has been missing.

What would it mean to give attention to personal spiritual development? The syllabus for a class in "Personal Spirituality" offered then at the seminary included theological reflection on topics like the divine-human relationship, images of God, God as Creator/provider, God as Love (lover/covenant/betrothal), God as one who suffers, yielding to God (*Gelassenheit*), following Jesus in life (discipleship), God as one who communes (Trinity).

The syllabus also included a practical component of sampling spiritual disciplines, such as presence (centering), presence (praising), a spirituality retreat, confession (opening), consciousness (*Examen*), forgiveness (releasing), forgiveness (holding), petition (asking), intercession, meditation, and discernment. Could this be a model for the church now?

A much longer "Proposal for Spiritual Disciplines" written by Smucker in 1985 was presented to the seminary board in meetings two years later, in March 1985. This is the document Smucker says faculty were "writing and rewriting parts of the proposal until we could all come to accept it."[41]

I will lift out key emphases in the proposal which I think are important to notice and build on. Smucker starts by deeply rooting the need for spiritual disciplines in theology, with his discussion of "basic freedom" in Anabaptist thought. "In Mennonite experience," he begins,

spiritual disciplines emerge from an understanding of the nature of the [C]hristian life. . . . For the Anabaptists a certain discipline (discipleship) was essential because of their view of God, human nature and the church. In their thought God is good, has created all things good, and does not compel anyone to do evil. God also created humans with a basic freedom; each person is . . . free "to choose good and evil, even as Adam" did. . . . Where there is choice disciplines are essential.[42]

Thus the need for spiritual disciplines grows out of an Anabaptist theological emphasis on the relative freedom of the will, on choice. Smucker goes on to describe Anabaptist spiritual formation:

God's nature and character are being stamped upon the person's character as s/he follows Jesus in life. The divine image is renewed; the knowledge of good and evil and the freedom of choice are increased. Thus good works are not to win divine approval but to cooperate with the divine will in the transformation of the inner core of the person's life.[43]

Key terms are *freedom, following Jesus in life*, and *transformation*. Here we can essentially see a theological definition of spiritual formation in the Anabaptist tradition. The emphasis is on decision (will) and action, the freedom to do the good, and cooperate with God. But such formation also stresses transformation of the inner core of a person's life.

Smucker has a fascinating description then of how discipline was practiced over the centuries in Anabaptist-Mennonite churches—and how we are now at the place where it is not practiced at all. Just these few paragraphs make the paper invaluable. Smucker says in part, regarding disciplines:

In later Mennonite experience [discipline] was expressed in a variety of ways. Theologically it was expressed in the concept of and teaching about discipleship. Formally or structurally it was expressed in the Mennonite practice of baptism, communion, church rules, function of the Deacons, sermons of exhortation, and in some cases excommunication. Informally there have been a variety of practices and expressions of piety in Mennonite life designed to help the individual and the church to be faithful "followers of Jesus," e.g., patterns of dress, simplicity of life, honesty, truthfulness, returning good for evil, regular Bible reading and prayer—all to help us live the godly life.[44]

Here we notice practices Smucker lists that no longer exist or are left only in vestigial form—practices we have observed in my grandmother's life: church rules, excommunication, patterns of dress, simplicity of life, regular Bible reading, and prayer.

The proposal describes our current reaction as Mennonites to the legalistic way discipline was enforced in an earlier time. That reaction often now means that we resist any mention of the word *discipline* at all. Smucker mentions that small groups have been one way we thought this accountability was happening but describes what I have also observed, that accountability doesn't necessarily go deep enough in those groups. Indeed he concludes: "*It seems likely in Mennonite congregational life that many persons, after the baptismal vows, do not experience being accountable to anyone in this life for their relationship with God or the church*" (my italics).[45] This is a realistic assessment of a current lack in our church experience, in our Mennonite Christian lives, stated more strongly than I am accustomed to, but extremely helpful because of its honesty.[46]

After Smucker describes how accountability is not happening anymore, and why it isn't, he stresses that the seminary program of spiritual disciplines has to be more "invitational"[47] than perhaps we as Mennonites have experienced disciplines in the past. The Anabaptists stressed freedom and voluntarism. Freedom needs to be stressed in practicing disciplines as well. So he concludes that we need to find new structures, "realistic structures," to do face-to-face accountability, and we need to stress the "invitational" aspect of this: "Just as God's call to life in the Spirit is invitational in nature so must spiritual disciplines be engaged in voluntarily. . . . Any endeavors in Discipleship and Spiritual Formation must make the 'invitational encounter' alive and vital. We must be confronted with the divine call to be transformed into the likeness of God."[48]

At the end Smucker proposes very specific new structures and practices to begin to work at disciplines at the seminary. These I believe can be added to or can replace some of the older structures and practices which have died out in the wider church. When coupled with our older themes and emphases, these spiritual practices can create a stronger foundation for Christian living in the twenty-first century. One of these practices is spiritual direction or spiritual mentoring. Smucker says,

> I believe we need disciplines or *practices* [italics mine] which encourage personal and corporate conversations about our life with God. One example of this is the practice of Spiritual Mentoring in which two individuals come together to reflect upon the one persons [sic] experience of and walk with God. . . . This may involve encouragement, confrontation, clarifying, supportive caring, praying together . . . etc.[49]

He mentions other helpful contemplative practices:

> It seems apparent in contemporary Mennonite experience that meditation, contemplation, interior prayer, intercessory prayer, centering prayer, journaling, solitude, spiritual direction (disciplines associated with Spiritual Formation which have come largely from the liturgical traditions) can be compatible with and complementary to the Mennonite concern for faithfulness which is inherent in the emphasis upon Discipleship. Baptism and church membership, following Jesus, mutual admonition, and mutual aid can be inspired and enhanced by contemplative prayer, solitude, and journaling; the deeds of discipleship can be inspired by the love that is kindled in the soul that contemplates God. And spiritual mentoring or spiritual friendship can indeed be a means of renewing one's baptismal vows, and a source of appropriate admonition and mutual care.[50]

This proposal for spiritual disciplines at AMBS could just as easily be called "Proposal for Spiritual Disciplines in the [Whole] Mennonite Church." The proposal seems to me to be a way forward for the entire church—to discover new practices and realistic structures for the God-life of modern Mennonites, to enhance and revitalize our discipleship.

Chapter Seven

BECOMING LIKE CHRIST INWARDLY AND OUTWARDLY

As I have said often in these pages and hopefully illustrated through my grandmother's life, Mennonites are in a new historical situation. The loss of the old agricultural-based way of life and way of formation needs to be recognized before Mennonites can move forward with new ways of spiritual formation. I have tried to describe the way life was then, a little about the shape of life now, and some of the new needs these changes raise. "No one can avoid being shaped by the shapes he moves among constantly."[1]

Because of the disappearance of these older forms of communal ethical spirituality, which were embedded in everyday life—the *land-based practices of previous generations*[2]—Mennonites have been moving from a "village" spirituality to a "city" spirituality; from a spirituality of "dwelling" or "place" to a spirituality of "seeking."[3]

The shift is also from a spirituality or spiritual formation that didn't need to be explicit, as Marlene Kropf says in her interview, to one we need to pay attention to. Therefore Mennonites are currently drawing on more ancient church formation tools and mining their own Anabaptist tradition in new ways.

As Mennonites and others shift from village spirituality to city spirituality, the change must be conscious and verbalized.

Delbert Wiens' description of the village spirituality among Mennonites, which I have referred to several times, continues below as he addresses its advantages and disadvantages:

> The church was the center of the [community] . . . knowledge and action and faith were integrated by the underlying cultural structure. This structure was absorbed by the growing child. . . . Since it was always being done, there was little need to set apart special times and places for doing it. . . . One then arrived at adulthood having absorbed the structure of the faith. . . .

Turning to disadvantes, Wiens says that these

> were largely the other side of the advantages. A structure so fully internalized could hardly be recognized for what it was. . . . [S]uch a culture is not aware of its own deeper grammar. . . . This was also true for the individual. When taken out of his supporting culture, he was often lost. For he had learned to go along with mores and morals presumed to be right because everyone he knew held them. Where they were not taken for granted, he often found it easier to go along with a new set. What he had learned in the village was not principles. He had really learned to fit in.[4]

Two things here to note: Mennonites now have to be more intentional, more explicitly person-oriented and inner-oriented in their spiritual formation of people. They are out in "the world" now and not in those old, sacred communities of "place." Mennonites need to learn to verbalize their own "deeper grammar" and are being pushed to do so by a new historical situation.

Second, many Mennonites, having learned simply to fit into their community, are not equipped to understand or articulate their own "grammar." Many who grew up this way take the values and practices for granted and do not understand how they can be unfamiliar Good News in the larger society.

Marlin Miller recognized a new situation, because he was away in Europe for a significant time and came back with new eyes. His life experience for an extended time was more one of displacement. "It is very significant that someone like Marlin Miller, who recognized the need for spirituality, was not doing so out of a fad mentality, but simply recognizing reality both negatively (a lack in his own faith community) and positively (the scriptural validity and value of the 'spiritual' tradition)'.[5]

Miller recognized a lack in his faith community by being "out of the sacred place." Others like Marlene Kropf also talk about a displacement experience of being outside their Mennonite communal structures, which pushed them toward new forms of spiritual growth.

Kropf says[6] that she learned that *one's own deep connection to God either has to be cultivated in adversity or intentionally in spiritual formation practices.* Since we cannot now depend on adversity always forcing people to depend on God, as was the case with the early Mennonite martyrs and is still often the case with Mennonites in developing countries, we need to be more intentional about spiritual formation practices.

Because we are having to cultivate spirituality more intentionally and consciously, we are looking for tools and resources. We are more in a seeking mode right now spiritually than in a dwelling mode. We found these tools and resources initially with Catholics in the 1970s and 1980s; now we are looking for them in our own tradition. We are shifting from the more activist-focused spirituality of the 1940s, '50s, and '60s to a Mennonite spirituality that includes an identification with Jesus in more than behavior. There is increasingly a realization that we don't only have to go to those other places outside our Mennonite tradition to find a piety to undergird our discipleship. We have so much of what we need in our own tradition.[7] Ongoing research is being done to find that spirituality in our own Anabaptist-Mennonite tradition.[8] This book is part of that wider search. I tried to find resources in my Mennonite immediate past, in local stories of women's lives. Others have been looking for resources in the sixteenth-century Anabaptist sources and elsewhere.

It is important to continue to look in the Mennonite tradition, as well as in other traditions, for roots and resources. Though the communally embedded agricultural Mennonite spiritual formation of my grandmother *was* mediated by "place" and Mennonites no longer live in those holy "places," Mennonites need to remember that this more traditional spirituality had the same *themes* the world needs now—mutual aid, simplicity, Gelassenheit, generosity, relationship, visiting, hospitality, feeding the enemy, separation from evil. The forms will be different, but the content will still be shaped by the same Gospel.

Then it was mediated by place, by clothes, and by physical separation in more isolated, contained communities. It was mediated by more outward things. Now it *has* to be more inward—because it isn't outward anymore. We *have* to make an inner transformation, have to focus on that. The heart of what we are trying to do in our Christian lives needs to be emphasized because we are living our faith right in the middle of what we used to call "the world," which used to be "out there." Now we are in it every day, and we each have to be stronger because we aren't always together, depending on the community to make a stand for us. Each of us has to have a connection to God. There is a new awareness of that, which first came from people in mission or urban ministries—Marlin Miller, Thelma Groff, Marcus Smucker, Marlene Kropf. It is no accident they all got into this when they returned from service overseas or in an inner city far removed from Mennonite rural community. People separated from place were the ones who started paying attention to this in the 1970s and 1980s.

It is now gradually dawning on the rest of us. For example, since we are doing more active peacemaking "out there," we feel a need to strengthen ourselves in the inner being. Ted Koontz has taught a course at AMBS called "Spirituality and Peacemaking" which talks about becoming peacemakers "from the inside out."[9] The inner emphasis is a logical necessity when we can no longer depend on the outer, on those around us believing the same thing. It is a logical need, to be stronger individually, as the community's form changes from less isolated "village" to "city." Our spirituality, our faith has to be more explicit and conscious. We have to know why we believe it and how to be articulate about it. This explains the more intensely inner focus of recent years.[10]

A major difference between my grandmother's life and mine is that I went farther away. I tried to take the community along to Ireland, but when it fell apart, I couldn't access God through it anymore. Marlene Kropf calls this "bankruptcy—you can operate on the communal capital as long as you have tightly knit communities" or can stay in those communities. I lost my access to God in Ireland when the community fell apart, because my access to God was only through the community. My connection to God was only communal. That is why we need our current emphasis on personal spirituality.

We don't want to lose that communal emphasis, but for it to survive we need to strengthen whatever communal ethos we have left from the inside out. We don't want to lose the realization that what we do with people and what we do with God are always interrelated. This has been our strength, and we need to value that.

This can be an important Mennonite contribution to the wider spiritual formation world right now, if we could accomplish this! Or if we could retain it from our past—for this book illustrates that in the early twentieth century, we kept piety and social nonconformity together. Can we continue to do so? With all this reemphasis on the inner, we may tend to think now that our faith doesn't have to be externalized at all. But that can be a misconception. Is it always Good News that we can look and act just like our neighbors?

Mennonites have often been able to keep inner and outer together. Let's not lose this! By putting "spirituality" under "discipleship" in the Mennonite *Confession of Faith*,[11] we as Mennonites are expressing an ongoing concern that things of the Spirit cannot be detached from following Jesus in life, from ethics. This is the main value that is in continuity with the past.

So what, after all we've been through in these stories of grandmothers and monks and mission and seminary, can we take into the future? I want to look now at the Mennonite spiritual themes we've started to talk about, those I believe can continue to be Good News in today's arrogant world. Hopefully these are not just Mennonite distinctives but central gospel values the Anabaptist/ Mennonite tradition has more or less successfully embodied already for centuries. We might need to embody them differently now, so I've started to think about how. It's really a conversation that needs to happen communally, not just through an individual author like me making proposals.

What is needed in a Mennonite spirituality for the twenty-first century? The following seem to me to be six key elements[12]: an everyday, embodied sacramentality; nonconformity; community; service; Gelassenheit or meekness; and the person of Jesus and the Bible.

When I first made this list, it was just that—a list of themes. My thesis advisors told me I had to make it more concrete and make some actual specific suggestions for action. I resisted putting concrete suggestions down—I felt that should be a communal process. In fact, I still believe a group of Mennonites of various ethnicities and ages and experiences should look at these themes and tell me if I got the six key ones down rightly and suggest their own ways of living them out.

But in 2003 my thesis advisors wouldn't let me graduate without suggestions. So I showed this list of themes to a small group of fellow Mennonites before I turned in the thesis, and they helped me brainstorm some ways we might practice these now. I will include one concrete suggestion for each of the following points. Each section begins with a theological statement in italics, a general discussion of the theme, and then subpoints. Although the six major themes are an attempt to be exhaustive, the sub-points are meant to be more suggestive, a springboard for further discussion.

An Everyday, Embodied Sacramentality

God is in the ordinary. Mennonite spirituality encompasses *every* activity and relationship, not just Sunday but during the week. Tom Finger claims that Anabaptists were very "sacramental" in their "efforts to embody divine grace in every activity and relationship."[13] Mennonites do not focus on magnificent churches or cathedrals, or on sacred spaces or sacred clothes, or on the Eucharist, in the sense that Catholic people express their sacramentality. Mennonites have had homely churches—more like everyday spaces—because of this belief that God is in the everyday, in the ordinary relationships they have in family and in community life.

My grandmother wore her covering every day because "her whole life was a prayer." Mennonite spirituality in her day was a way of life, a seamless whole, encompassing every day and every activity. This reflected, at its best, an integrated life, with (a related word) an unusual integrity. Today Mennonites are still serious about embodying our faith in our whole life, not just on Sunday mornings.

This way of life has held together social and personal piety. In my grandmother's life, for instance, piety was expressed in very concrete social ways—helping neighbors, feeding and housing refugees, living a communal life nonconformed to the world in terms of clothing, adornment, and morality—as well as in personal piety: devotional Bible reading, private prayer, and hymn-singing. In my description of Mennonite spirituality today, I want also to stress equally the communal and personal dimensions of piety. One suggestion: When doing evangelism in our local communities, we need to always stress the importance of orthopraxy as well as orthodoxy, right practice as well as right belief. Marlin Miller gives examples:

> Jesus' followers are called to be reconciled with each other even before bringing their offerings to God, to remain faithful in marriage, to tell the truth in public as well as in private, to practice a new pattern of justice, and to show love to those considered to be enemies of one's own nation, class, profession, and kind. Such actions will be publicly visible. . . . Jesus incarnated this quality of life and called his disciples to do the same.[14]

Earthy

Mennonite spirituality has been very "earthy" (definition: "consisting of or resembling earth or soil; pertaining to or characteristic of this world") compared to the more other-worldly, celibate, silent Catholic tradition I encounter when I go on spiritual retreats to monasteries or spirituality centers. Mennonites will always have a more earthy, incarnational form of spirituality that embraces family life and every day life fully. There are not levels of sanctity, one lay and one "religious." One suggestion: Think about and ask God about how your own family life reflects God's life right now. I tried to do that in a sermon many years ago, and I also found a book by a British Catholic woman, called *Motherhood and God*, extremely helpful.[15]

Serious about our faith

Plain clothes then meant "getting serious about [her] faith" to my grandmother. It was an outward sign of a significant spiritual reality. How might we now signal "getting serious" about our adult faith, if we don't want to wear different clothes?[16] One suggestion: to make a commitment to spiritual disciplines and a spiritual director or spiritual friend. This means leaders providing tools to do this, so I will list a few here. The book *Praying with the Anabaptists*[17] can be used to teach some classic spiritual practices (practices are found at the end of each chapter). A book called *Sleeping with Bread*[18] can be used to teach a discipline called "Examen of Consciousness" (The Examen is a discipline to help notice God in one's daily life experiences).

Pastors in other traditions are also beginning to experiment with intentionally teaching their congregants to pray. I have recently seen a Doctor of Ministry thesis by a Presbyterian pastor subtitled "The Use of Spiritual Disciplines in a Presbyterian Congregation."[19] Kent Groff, founder of Oasis Ministries and former professor and pastor, has a great book of spiritual exercises called *Active Spirituality: A Guide for Seekers and Ministers* that I've used in congregational leadership.[20] The exercises are for groups, for committees in the church, for pastoral leaders.

Denominations can learn much from each other in this common task. People in congregations can also be encouraged and trained to have a spiritual friendship with one other person. I am increasingly concerned that one-size-fits-all corporate mentoring through sermons is not enough. People need personal mentoring. Pastors themselves can be encouraged to choose a trained spiritual director and be in direction. This is a requirement for priests in some Catholic archdiocese.

The importance of a rhythm of life, including the Sabbath

In my grandmother's life, the rhythms of work and rest, of engagement and disengagement (Sabbath), of activity and lulls, happened naturally, according to nature's patterns. I have heard a farmer say, "When the hay's ready, you work till it's all in the barn, no matter how late at night." I presume that the opposite was also true about the times nature was dormant, in the winter. The activity level might have slowed down a little then.

However, even if this is a nostalgic misconception, even if they were busy too, we need to deal with our own reality—the frenzied pace of life for many of us. This is a key spiritual issue for us as modern people, and the church often is not addressing it. As non-agrarian people we don't have "lulls" anymore, so we have to create them, create regular breaks or retreat or disengagement time. This might be one of the hardest practices or disciplines to manage in our current day, when "wasting time with God" is not a priority. What is Sabbath for us, if it isn't Sunday dinners and visiting afterwards anymore? Sabbath is more a rhythm of life, of action and contemplation, ministry and reflection, that is desperately needed in our world today.

According to Tilden Edwards in *Spiritual Friend*,[21] reclaiming the rhythm of work and rest could be the key task of the church today, helping to reclaim an everyday sacramentality. One suggestion: put aside Sabbath time each day for prayer and each week for a day of rest when you put aside your to-do lists and enjoy just "being." And put aside longer retreat times in a regular rhythm. I try to take a day or two a month. Some Catholic people take a month a year for retreat. The regular rhythm is important. Take prime time to do this, not leftover time. Put it in your date book ahead of time, and be careful not to let it go, just as we put aside a tithe *before* we spend our money, not afterward when there's nothing left!

Nonconformity

If we are conformed to Christ, we will not be conformed to many aspects of our world which are broken and sinful. Separation from the world was a theme expressed in my grandmother's life in her plain clothes, in her separate, German, language, in her physical separation in a bounded community of like-minded people. This separation has also been called "nonconformity." However, the theme of being "conformed to Christ," and therefore nonconformed to the world, might look different now. In a book on preparing for baptism called *Welcoming New Christians*, the authors state that unless we make a conscious decision, we'll be formed by our world rather than by the mind of Christ: "All of us are suffering the destructive effects of our fragmented world. Unless we make a conscious decision to the contrary, we become formed—conformed and deformed—into the image of our broken world."[22]

I've mentioned the issues of violence, greed, addiction to busyness and being alienated from nature before in these pages. All of these are symptoms of the brokenness of the world. Nonconformity to all this is still crucial and might include the following:

Simplicity

In my grandmother's life simplicity was expressed in plain clothes and simplicity of architecture, i.e., the plain meeting house she worshipped in at Salford. Now, in addition to outward simplicity, which we rarely practice, it might mean a need for silence and solitude. Spending time in silence is a key way to experience simplicity in one's life.[23] A group like Mennonites, who emphasize community as much as we do, has to have an emphasis as well on being alone with God in silence. Cistercian (Trappist) monks emphasize this by limiting talk, so that they can be alone even in the company of each other. Dietrich Bonhoeffer[24] says "he who cannot be alone, should not be in community" and vice versa. I go to our Mennonite retreat centers, such as Laurelville and Spruce Lake, and have a hard time finding a place to be alone. There are many many rooms to be together in, to sleep together in, to play games together in, to worship together in, but I can't find any rooms to be alone in.

An article called "Solitude"[25] by Henri Nouwen in *Sojourners* magazine helped me tremendously when I was living in an intentional community in Dublin, Ireland. Nouwen helped me understand what was wrong in our little community—the constant togetherness did not allow for adequate time alone with oneself or with God. I realized this especially after meeting Brother Eoin de Bhaldraithe and his community and noticing how little they talk. In fact, he told us they didn't talk at all for the first fifteen years that he was a Cistercian. This was before Vatican II loosened the rules a little bit. They understood the need for preserving individual communion with God, after a thousand years or more of practicing community.

One suggestion: We need places to be alone. We need to invest money in creating places to be alone—create simple prayer rooms in our churches with the only furnishing a window (or windows) and a comfortable chair for looking out at the beauty of nature; create hermitage-style buildings at our retreat centers; create retreat centers in the middle of our communities designed for being alone. Or we can adapt already-existing spaces for spending time alone with God. Whole groups can be in silence if a retreat director just helps set those parameters.[26]

At the London Mennonite Center, they have built a hut on stilts in the backyard, to be a mini-hermitage. Once a person goes in there, she or he is not disturbed by others. Ideally, such places will also have food preparation, a way of eating in silence, and places to sleep, so that one can be in silence for more than a couple hours.

Meditative tasks

When Mennonites were primarily rural and lived and worked on a farm, they had tasks that lent themselves more to meditation. Now there is the need for carving out more meditation time, more time when we aren't being stimulated, because now the tasks we do are not as repetitive as plowing fields or chopping vegetables might have been. Marcus Smucker said that when he was growing up as an Amish boy, he spent time driving the tractor and memorized Scripture at the same time. Now if you are driving a car, you often cannot disengage your mind enough to do something like that because it would be dangerous. The alertness level has to be higher. We pride ourselves on multitasking. Maybe the closest we get to "driving a tractor" is when we're on the treadmill at the gym. One author talks about the importance of "those quiet activities that free the mind for meditation," such as raking leaves.[27]

One suggestion: Another way to be "nonconformed" in our current world is to do one thing at a time every now and then. Don't wash dishes and talk on the phone at the same time. Turn off the radio in the car. Take a break from multitasking every once in a while.

Being discerning about technology

This was briefly referred to in my story about my grandparents and the radio. What kind of a stance do we take now on the influence of media, technology? We need to have many discerning conversations about this. In *Practicing our Faith*, Mennonites are cited as an example of a group which has not chosen a "hair-shirt" asceticism yet has continued to raise questions of "right technology."[28] Let's not lose this! The authors of *Practicing our Faith* continue,

> We live in a world where economic life is dramatically driven by technological development. Whereas some assume that salvation is to be found in technology and others see technology as inevitably destructive and beyond our control, Mennonites can help us perceive our power to create tools/technology as requiring the same development of ethical wisdom as other forms of power.[29]

Today, in addition to controlling the radio, we must also be discerning about use of television, cell phones, computers, video games, and more. We try to be careful about the formation of our children, but Madison Avenue never sleeps! This is such a large task that we need a whole community, a village, to raise our children. One suggestion: I try not to look at my e-mail before I pray in the morning. Once I turn on my computer, it is very seductive!

Separating from evil

The German language once helped promote a sense of "separation from the world" by language and culture. We don't speak German anymore, and other cultural groups and languages abound in our congregations (praise God, in my small congregation there are people who speak Swahili, Chinese, Vietnamese, Luo among other languages). Now separation means not so much physical and cultural separation as "separating from evil." Mennonites could do this, as mentioned earlier, by questioning the constant activity and busy-ness that the Devil loves. In *Celebration of Discipline*, Richard Foster says: "In contemporary society our Adversary majors in three things:

noise, hurry, and crowds. . . . Psychiatrist C. G. Jung once remarked, 'Hurry is not of the Devil; it is the Devil.'"[30] Constant stimulation and busyness makes it hard to hear or respond to God in our lives. We need to slow down to save our souls.

Besides addressing busyness and over stimulation, separation or nonconformity might also mean questioning the materialistic focus of American society and the reliance on violence that is part of our culture. I recommend evangelical leader Ron Sider's books for further exploration—he has written much better than I ever could on these two themes of the Christian response to materialism and violence.[31]

One suggestion: In terms of separation from materialism, our practice of not working and not shopping (earning and spending money) on Sunday mornings to go to church is counter-cultural. I try not to shop Sunday afternoon either, but I am not always successful at that. To practice "separation" from violence, Mennonites have sponsored a gun recall in Elkhart, Indiana. Mennonite voices have been heard in the debate about gun control laws in Pennsylvania, particularly in Philadelphia.

Community

God and our experience with each other are interrelated. What was community then and what is it now? It continues to be key—but back then it meant seeing each other every day. Now when we "see" each other more through e-mail than in person, I am beginning to wonder if the congregation, the local gathering of God's people, doesn't become even more important than it was in my grandmother's day. How can we find new ways to be in face-to-face relationships that mean something more than passing each other on Sunday morning?

We also need to look more at what is at the heart of community. We need to stress again the importance of the actual physical gathering of the community *and* also its inner meaning. Ron Sawatazky reports that "At the beginning of his book, *A Different Drum*, M. Scott Peck said, 'In and through community lies the salvation of the world.'" Sawatzky adds that in an interview "Peck was asked to explain that statement. Among other things he said: 'We consider community to be a group of people that have made a commitment to learn how to communicate with each other at an ever more deep and authentic level.'"[32]

An investment of time and a willingness to learn to listen will be necessary. A level of commitment we don't often see in modern life will be necessary, as well as a level of skill in relationships and truth-telling and forgiveness, in order for meaningful community to develop in congregations. Some new structures such as two-person spiritual friendships or spiritual formation groups might be helpful. David Augsburger, in *Dissident Discipleship*, calls the practice of Christian community one of eight core Christian practices and says that it requires, in his terms, "Stubborn Loyalty."[33]

I said in chapter five that the synagogue and the Torah became more crucial when Israelites were forced off the land. They were both portable. For Mennonites today, perhaps the congregation (and later I'll talk about the Bible) needs to take even more priority than it has in the recent past. The congregation is a primary locus for community building. A primary purpose of God's people is to learn to love. The congregation is a school of love.

We need to recognize the interrelationship between our experience of God's love and our experience with each other. Marcus Smucker grounds community in theology in his "Proposal." He says that how we experience our common life is just as important to our formation as how we experience private prayer.

> Crucial is the nature of the face to face encounters in the corporate life of the people of God, i.e., the manner in which decisions are made together, the nature of the group life of a congregation. . . . In discipleship and spiritual formation the experience of God in personal and corporate life are vitally interrelated.[34]

For Mennonites, our relationships are "holy." They are what we endow with supreme spiritual significance, and we take them with the seriousness Catholics take the "Host" in the celebration of the Eucharist. We take each other as seriously as we take God, one Mennonite has said. Mennonites continue to believe centrally in community and to commit ourselves to being in regular relationship with specific people. This forms a kind of covenant community, a covenant to stick it out with these relationships when they get uncomfortable, too.

Approaches to self and conflict

New approaches to self are crucial. As long as we were in self-contained communities where everyone played by the same rules, we didn't have to develop ego strength. When we are in cities or in jobs or in mission settings where some self-preservation skills are necessary, we struggle as Mennonites to find good theology for this. Smucker's thesis combining self-realization and self-sacrifice is an important study toward this end.[35] My grandmother had trouble negotiating a conflict situation with her supervisor when she went out to work. I had trouble in Ireland with self-preservation when I'd been schooled in self-denial. We need strengthening of the inner self as part of our spiritual formation agenda as Mennonites encounter more conflicts within our communities and encounter life outside the Christian community. One suggestion: Study authors like Joann Wolski Conn[36] and Marcus Smucker who have integrated their theories of personal development and spiritual growth.

Visiting

I was struck in my research by the importance of what Beulah Hostetler calls the "biblical work of visiting."[37] I heard often in my grandmother's story and the stories of other women of "Sunday visiting." Food was prepared the day ahead or stored in freezers, in anticipation of visiting on Sunday. Visiting also happened to comfort those whose loved ones had died, or to provide other forms of mutual care, i.e. to the sick.

We might need to find new patterns of meeting each other and of mutual care that fit our age. One suggestion: We could go back to the every-other-week Sunday church service I learned about in my research, leaving the alternate weeks free for visiting among members of the congregation and eating in each other's homes. We tend to hope that happens on top of our other schedules, and it doesn't seem to be happening. We can't add another thing. But by taking something away, such as a church service every other Sunday, we could create a space for visiting. There would be historical precedent for this. This every-other-week practice could be structured so that table groups would be formed if we didn't want to just leave it to chance that people would actually visit each other.

Mutual accountability

This value has been promoted in recent years by Marcus Smucker and Marlene Kropf[38] in articles calling for each believer to be involved in a regular form of accountability—a spiritual friendship with one other person. This important Mennonite theme has also been called "giving and receiving counsel," a promise to be open to the counsel of each other, to be open to hearing God through each other. Spiritual friendship, where two people covenant together to be accountable and open with their spiritual lives, is a necessary structure to promote giving and receiving counsel in our modern era.

One suggestion: Start programs in our local congregations to walk with people in groups of two's as they learn how to have spiritual friendships that aren't about advice-giving but about truly listening to the other person's walk with God. I am currently trying to do that as a pastor.[39] I have learned that it also necessitates some teaching about how to listen to other people at a soul level. It is helpful as well to have people experience *receiving* this kind of attentive listening so they know how to replicate it with another.

Eating together

One of my grandmother's strongest memories is of a long table filled with people and food. For modern-day Mennonites, eating together is still a form of communion. Eating together and sharing food is symbolic of giving and receiving nurture. We do it when somebody has a baby; we do it when somebody dies; we send canned beef overseas. We do it almost instinctually. The *More-with-Less*[40] cookbook and its variants are the Mennonite bestsellers. Eating together is a sharing of God's nourishment with each other.[41] "We are each other's bread and wine," as the hymn writer says.

Eating together can also be a form of evangelism when we invite others to eat with us. We can recognize that we are promoting the kingdom of God, we are serving God, when we spend time shopping for food, cooking food, eating with our families and with friends. We are not taking time away from God, away from church when we do this. (Just don't make women do it alone, because they aren't home any more than men now.) My sister-in-law used to run a local tea room that was part of the glue that held the local community together. It was also an outreach ministry, providing salt and light and leavening to a wider community than just the local congregation. Gordon Houser, an editor of the denominational paper has said, "National Public Radio . . . reported that according to one study, the single factor that consistently corresponds with whether or not a student succeeds at school is if that student eats dinner with family members." Houser suggests that

As we think about the many ways our culture affects our lives and the education of our children, we tend to think of the effects of television, movies, music, advertising. These all affect us, I'm sure. But we overlook the simple ways we can exercise great good, such as eating together. Given current practices, this may be a radical act. Many families rush from one activity to another, grabbing something to eat on the run. Or schedules force them to eat at different times. Or they eat in the living room in front of the TV. Such practices have their negative effects. Sitting down together at the dinner table, once a fairly common occurrence, now requires a certain intentionality. If we do not make the effort, it likely will not happen. . . . Except for occasional potlucks, churches today rarely eat together. And now even families seem to have trouble eating together. The promotion of such a practice would seem to fit nicely with Mennonite practice. We might even follow Jesus' example and make it a method of evangelism. Let's pull up a chair and eat together.[42]

One suggestion: Support and encourage families to keep at least one night a week as "sacred," for an extended meal together, like the Jews celebrate a sabbath meal Friday night. (It would help if all the families in the church did it the same night.) Eat together as churches on a regular basis, especially with visitors.

Believers baptism

The importance of an adult choice for faith, of voluntarism, an emphasis on the will and free choice, have been theological underpinnings for believers' baptism. Mennonites have always emphasized the ability to "do the good." They have not wanted to use depravity as an "excuse" for not following Jesus in life. In terms of spiritual formation, this emphasis on freedom means, in fact, that Mennonites both need to stress disciplines, but in a very invitational way, not a legalistic way, and learn to be invitational, as God is invitational. One suggestion: We could offer a variety of practices and disciplines, and make sure people are free to choose. That is one reason I have hesitated to say *We should do this or that*. God has made a variety of people and given us free will. Some forms of prayer, for example, work better for some people than others. My suggestions after each point are just that—suggestions.

Service

We get to know Christ, not just as we learn about him, but as we live the same life of service that he did. Mennonites have recognized that we are spiritually formed by being in community, as much as by being in prayer, and the same is true for mission and service. A generation of Mennonite leaders was formed by serving as conscientious objectors during World War II, often in mental hospitals. Service assignments with Mennonite Central Committee in Latin America have changed people immeasurably.[43]

Love-in-action

The practice of very concrete mutual aid within the congregation and concrete service outside the congregation is a central value, almost the defining value, among Mennonites. In my grandmother's day it involved feeding, clothing, giving haircuts to and even parenting recent immigrants. Mennonites specialize in love-in-action, love-in-concrete-form even now in our local churches and through Mennonite Central Committee and

Mennonite Disaster Service (new forms for our mutual aid). We practice "love in the form of sticky buns" (see chapter two). This is another way Mennonites practice an everyday embodied spirituality, by being very practical rather than just talking about faith.

It reminds me of another Mennonite woman who agreed to be a prayer partner for me as summer Bible school teacher but also made supper for us so I could get there on time easier—she expressed the genius of Mennonite love-in-action. One suggestion: Every Mennonite young person or retiree could be encouraged to give one year of service away from their local community.

Footwashing

Footwashing has been practiced by Mennonites of my grandmother's day until the present. It is a symbol of service, often combined with twice-yearly communion, that continues to have meaning. It graphically portrays Mennonites' stance of being servants, as Christ commanded, rather than lording it over others. One suggestion: Continue this practice on a regular basis, while teaching its meaning to newcomers.

Hospitality to needy "strangers"

At their dinner table my grandmother's family hosted the Jewish peddler who came to sell them household goods as well as the tramps who came almost daily during the American Depression. Is this a value that endures from her life that now takes different forms? By putting this value together with another old Mennonite term, *Niedrigkeit* (lowliness),[44] this value could now be seen as expressed in Mennonites' concern for the mentally handicapped. Franconia Conference Mennonites started an agency called Indian Creek Foundation that has served hundreds of people with developmental disabilities. Thousands of volunteer hours are also provided by local Mennonites who spend time with people with disabilities. Staying close to the "poor in spirit" and "welcoming the stranger" are values that need to continue. One suggestion: Find a local agency that serves people with disabilities or single homeless Moms (i.e. Bridge of Hope, based in eastern Pa.) and volunteer once a month, in a way that brings you into close contact with one particular person. Develop a meaningful relationship of give and take with that person.

Peacemaking

Peacemaking was once practiced in enclosed communities. My grandmother's brothers were conscientious objectors, but they never had to leave their communities to defend their position. Now Ted Koontz says, "The issue is how we can *be* and *become* authentic peacemakers, from the inside out."[45] As modern Mennonites practice peacemaking in more conflictual situations—for instance, as teams who intervene in the Israeli-Palestinian conflict—there is a need for a deep inner spirituality to sustain their peacemaking over the long haul. One suggestion: Our training programs for peace need to include worship and prayer as much as methods for nonviolent action. We are already doing this with Christian Peacemaker Teams and with courses like Ted Koontz's at AMBS. We have built in worship as part of peacemaking. We don't separate the two.

Discipleship or following Jesus

This continues to be a central theme now as it was implicit in my grandmother's life and community. However, Marcus Smucker helps us begin to redefine discipleship in terms of the "concrete realities of our daily lives" (i.e., in terms of the new historical situation) as modern American Mennonites, not just in terms of martyrdom as in the sixteenth century. His definition includes a new awareness of the importance of "being with Jesus, an essential part of discipleship, [which] includes time for prayer, reflection, meditation, learning to think and feel with Jesus' concern for the world, as well as accepting Jesus' personal interest in one's own life."[46] These are all inner-focused, "being"-focused, to complement the activist and outer focus of our spirituality of radical obedience. Arnold Snyder says: "Anabaptist spirituality, in continuity with the mainstream Christian spiritual tradition, refused to rest either on quietistic piety on the one hand, or on ethical activism on the other."[47] He believes that while "discipleship" was a crucial ingredient in Anabaptist spirituality, an understanding which sees discipleship merely as "obedience to the Lord's commands" bypasses crucial steps in the Anabaptist conception of the spiritual life. Ethics (that is, the "ought" that calls us to discipleship) holds out the end to be achieved in the form of concrete command: love your enemies, for example. In order for that command *to take root in one's life, however, the demand must be planted first in the inmost being as a spiritual call that demands a response.* . . . It is a vital spiritual life, not ethical vigilance, which makes disciples. . . [italics mine].

Elaborating, Snyder proposes that

Anabaptist spirituality does not ignore *the deeply personal transformation that must take place in the depth of individual lives.* Walking in the discipleship of love implies a deep spiritual struggle and growth, but the means of growth go against the current of technical control or personal mastery. Rather, growth in the Christian life comes with continuing dependence on the spiritual resources available to the believer, among which prayer (personal and corporate) and worship with the believing community remain primary [italics mine].[48]

Snyder's statements help to explain why a shift in discipleship is taking place, a new realization by Mennonites, based on having tried to live out discipleship without an explicit reliance on the Holy Spirit, that a better balance of inner and outer piety, of being and of doing, is needed. One suggestion: Don't use the word *discipleship* alone for a while; it has become almost like a slogan without specific content. Talk as well about *following Jesus in the concrete realities of our daily lives.* Then help individuals figure out what those current realities are for each of them and what following Jesus means in their specific circumstances, by providing spiritual direction.

A book which deals well with discipleship in the modern world is John Martin's *Ventures in Discipleship.*[49] It also teaches a practice or spiritual discipline in each chapter. This book could be used as a twenty-three-week sermon series with follow-up in Sunday school classes and small mid-week group meetings.

Gelassenheit or Meekness

We are creatures. I wondered if this was such a central category that it deserved a separate heading. I decided it did, because Gelassenheit can be expressed in all the categories: in relationship to God, to others, to the world.

Gelassenheit in relationship to God

This is the concept of "letting go of control," of "patience,"[50] of "yieldedness to uncreated God," that sixteenth-century Anabaptists borrowed from medieval mysticism and have specialized in ever since.

One suggestion: Begin to re-use this "beautiful word *Gelassenheit*" as Walter Klaassen calls it, for the way it can unify our inner and outer life in accordance with the nonviolent Cross of Jesus. Also as Klaassen suggests, rebaptize the word "nonresistance . . . living without weapons [without internally or externally controlling our surroundings] and fill it with [the spiritual meaning of the word *Gelassenheit* which includes inner surrender to God and patience]."[51]

Gelassenheit in relationship to others

In the Mennonite *Confession of Faith* the term *Gelassenheit* "has to do with radical openness to knowing God *and* to doing God's will" [italics mine].[52] Surrender to God and yielding to others are both expressions of Gelassenheit. "Letting go" takes shape in the outward, social realm as well as in the inner, mystical realm, expressing itself in concrete, practical ways, in community. Gelassenheit was often called "meekness" in my growing-up years. In my grandmother's story it was expressed by her father in giving away things and loaning money that never came back.

Now it might be illustrated by my son's letting a member of the opposing cross-country team win by seconds because the opponent lost his way on the running course and my son showed him the way and lost a couple seconds' advantage. He didn't do this because he wanted to lose! He did it because he forgot himself and wanted to help the visitor who was lost. However, Gelassenheit in relation to others needs very careful, Jesus-based definition, so as not to become mere stagnation or docility, particularly for Mennonite women. Jesus enjoyed sparring with women who seemed to know who they were in the Gospels (John 4).

Gelassenheit is a stance that comes at the end of a long process (Jesus was still asking God about alternatives in the Garden of Gethsemane); the process cannot be foreclosed. "Letting go" is only something that can be done after "taking hold of" one's life. One cannot let go of a self one does not have. It is not a quick goal that happens because of fear of developing as a person.[53] Jesus, in John 13:3-5, *"knowing that the Father had given all things into his hands, and that he had come from God and was going to God*, got up from the table, took off his outer robe, and tied a towel around himself . . . and began to wash the disciples' feet" (italics mine). One suggestion: As in teaching about conflict, use theories of spiritual development that build not only on Scripture but on psychological growth models compatible with Christian faith, for instance, those of Joann Wolski Conn and Marcus Smucker.[54]

Gelassenheit in relationship to the world

This is the opposite of the arrogance in our war filled world today. Mennonites have been able to link Gelassenheit as nonresistance to evil, with Gelassenheit as mystical stance toward God in their martyr or costly spirituality. Gelassenheit helped produce "a spirituality shaped by the ethical imperative to follow Jesus at all costs."[55] "Cost," yielding to others, not retaliating, even if it costs one's life, has been part of the Mennonite heritage.

I am noticing however, that we now have a more hopeful view in the United States about participation in the "world" outside our communities, than we did in the sixteenth century. One suggestion: One person translates Gelassenheit into "yielding life and possessions to God to be used in ministry in the church and world."[56] We can teach Gelassenheit as a "freeing for ministry" rather than as primarily a renunciation of the created world or a desire for martyrdom, even as we recommit ourselves to the giving up of all violence and to active peace-making.

The Person of Jesus and the Bible

To be conformed to Christ, to be formed by Christ, we need to spend very significant time with his words and in his presence, corporately and privately. I put this last—it could also have gone first—to give it priority. I want to stress the importance of Jesus because I am convinced of the centrality of Jesus and of the encounter with the Risen Christ through the Scriptures as a way to anchor Mennonites (and all Christians) in this Dark Night transitional time. Nelson Kraybill, at the time president of AMBS, said the "church ... must be centered on Jesus. ... Transforming ministry requires sustained encounter with God made known in Jesus Christ. ... When the risen Lord is the center of our lives, the Spirit will empower us to speak and act in ways that honor the One who shows us the face of God."[57] The centrality of Jesus Christ is not an unfamiliar theme to Mennonite-Anabaptists, who grew out of medieval movements practicing the imitation of Christ (*imitatio Christi*), according to Kenneth Davis' book on Anabaptism and asceticism.[58]

Finding a centering rather than a fracturing experience

"Finding a centering rather than a fracturing experience" is how one AMBS seminary student described what happened as he worked on spiritual formation.[59] Finding a centering experience is key. That is what the contemplative disciplines and contemplative prayer do for us. Some people find themselves in a tremendous balancing act, juggling their lives, family and profession. They need something to hold everything together—a deep anchoring in Christ. Centering prayer or contemplative prayer allow us to center in on our experience with God, become anchored in Jesus, as a way to give some coherence to an increasingly fractured existence.

In my grandmother's life, this coherence was provided by an ordered life that centered around a particular place that never changed for her. The place we meet God now is often "in Jesus" through the contemplative disciplines. Some Mennonites are using these now as spiritual formation tools—silence, solitude, daily personal prayer time, spiritual direction, contemplative/ listening prayer, lectio divina. These are needed not so much because of continuity with my grandmother's life, but because of a radical discontinuity, a Dark Night, which calls for more apophatic forms.

One suggestion: Teach people in Sunday school how to practice listening prayer and lectio divina. Also offer special weeks of prayer where people commit to reading a Scripture daily, meeting daily for half-an-hour with a spiritual director and meeting with a group for faith-sharing at the end of the week.[60] Take Sunday school classes on weekend retreats following the suggested retreat outlines in the book *Soul Care: How to Plan and Guide Inspirational Retreats*.[61] We need a concerted congregational effort to help people learn to pray, to listen to and talk to God, to read Scripture in a listening mode (lectio divina), to ask, What is God saying to me today through this Scripture? And we need to accompany them as spiritual friends or in spiritual direction as they try to pray.

Being formed by Scripture

I saw the Bible as the focus of my grandmother's life and spirituality, including an emphasis on the Sermon on the Mount. This emphasis then could lead to lectio divina now, or a daily Bible reading on a Mennonite web-page. It would be good if we as Mennonites would have a common daily prayer with a common Scripture. A Mennonite focus on the Bible would need to specialize in Jesus' life and the Sermon on the Mount but not exclude more mystical emphases found in places like the Gospel of John.

I have described how the Bible was emphasized at AMBS and in the writings of people like Arnold Snyder. For instance, Marcus Smucker and Willard Swartley saw the importance of starting a "Biblical Spirituality" course at AMBS, and Mennonites need to look more closely at the content of this course.[62] Marlin Miller refers to "A Genuine Biblical Spirituality"[63] as the title of his article on Mennonite spirituality. Arnold Snyder also makes much of the biblical bases of Anabaptist spirituality. Snyder says, in the introduction to the *Biblical Concordance of the Swiss Brethren, 1540:*

The memorization and internalization of selected works of Scripture suggests an ancient spiritual discipline that long predates Anabaptism and the Protestant Reformation. It is plain to see from Anabaptist prison testimonies, letters and hymns that the concrete language of the Bible, learned, repeated, and internalized, shaped the everyday consciousness and language of the Anabaptists.

Snyder explains that

Seen against the background of the Protestant laity approaching Scripture through the filter of catechism and confession, it can be said that the manner in which the Anabaptists appropriated Scripture recalls more the *ancient monastic tradition of "lectio divina" than it does the practice of the general Protestant laity* [my italics]. In the ancient tradition of the desert fathers, specific passages of the Bible were memorized and internalized to provide practical guidance for those who had committed themselves to following Christ's will in obedience. The object of the earliest practice of *lectio divina* was to be able to live in the words of the Bible, to soak them up, and to put them into practice.

Snyder suggests that

Ideally, the words of God were committed to memory for continual "rumination" (to be "chewed upon"). For all that was jettisoned from the Roman Catholic tradition, the Anabaptist way of reading, hearing, and remembering the Bible recalls this ancient practice and tradition of ruminating upon Scripture to practice what has been learned.[64]

I suggest this as a way forward for modern Mennonites—a practice—spiritual formation by means of immersion in the biblical text, "shap[ing our] every day consciousness." One suggestion: use the *Anabaptist Prayerbook* to immerse ourselves as a community in the same scriptures each day. The book called *Spiritual Traditions for the Contemporary Church* points out that *The Book of Common Prayer* was written as a way to unify the

Episcopal Church around a spiritual focus.[65] It was a communal—*common*—prayerbook. That's what we need now for ourselves. The *Anabaptist Prayerbook* readings could be supplemented by other denominations' lectionary readings so that we could feel united with the worldwide church.

Sing and playing hymns

Singing and playing hymns, especially Pietist hymns which focused on devotion to Jesus, were important to my grandmother and others of her generation. Marlene Kropf and Ken Nafziger point to hymn-singing now as one of the primary ways Mennonites pray.[66] This is a practice that needs to continue because it centers us on worshipping God, spending time with Jesus, in an intellectual as well as an emotional mode. One suggestion: Communal singing is not a skill that is easily learned; it is no longer practiced in the larger North American culture. We need intentional musical mentoring for newcomers among us.

Jesus

A relationship with the person of Jesus is equally as important as following him in life. As God calls Mennonites deeper and deeper into community and mission, God is also calling us deeper into the Jesus-life—a life of prayer—*and* following. We need to focus on Hans Denck's second line: "No one can truly follow Christ unless he first knows Him." Behind the discipleship language is the life and Person of Jesus. We need to keep getting back to that as the core. We need to keep coming back to the question: How does Jesus' life, death, and resurrection take shape within us and among us, in an inner as well as an outer way? We need to add an equal emphasis on prayer/ relating to the Person of Jesus onto the themes of community, service, Gelassenheit, and separation from evil which have been so crucial to Mennonites' understanding of the Christian faith.[67]

Conclusion

Spirituality is necessarily a way of life, a life that is a life of prayer and following Jesus. That is the genius of Mennonite spirituality—it *is* a way of life. Mennonite spirituality is something we do (ethics), together (community). It is ethically specific and communal. Mennonites live the Sermon on the Mount, as a corporate people. It is a way of life in a group, an everyday sacramentality, based on Jesus' life, death, and resurrection. We need to learn this about our own deeper grammar to live in a culture that speaks another "language."

However, I believe that what Mennonite spirituality is becoming is also important. Some of the new elements include the need to incorporate the ancient practice of spiritual friendship, spiritual conversation, spiritual direction to bolster spiritual conversation within the church;[68] the need to recapture an emphasis on personal inner transformation, on the new birth and the transforming power of prayer and the Holy Spirit; the need for Sabbath practice to be reemphasized (not because it is Anabaptist, but because it is deeply biblical and the present century needs it); and finally, the need to refocus on knowing the Person of Jesus, in addition to following Jesus. I am convinced of the centrality of Jesus, as I said earlier, and the centrality of the encounter with the Risen Christ through the Scriptures, as a way to anchor us all in this transitional time.

Stanley Hauerwas, professor of theological ethics at Duke University Divinity School, put it this way in a consultation on interchurch relations in 2004: "What you [Mennonites] bring to the table is an extraordinary rethinking of Christian theology, and the great discovery at the heart of your movement was simply, Jesus. . . . Michael Sattler looks kind of simple next to Martin Luther, but that is part of the genius."[69]

David Augsburger, in his *Dissident Discipleship*,[70] talks about eight core practices of Christians. They are: radical attachment to Jesus; stubborn loyalty in community; tenacious serenity (what I have called Gelassenheit); habitual humility; resolute nonviolence; concrete service; authentic witness; and subversive spirituality. He starts the whole list with radical attachment to Jesus.

I was into "radical," though I'm not sure I would've called it "radical attachment to Jesus," when I was in my twenties. I might have called it radical living out the gospel. Or living the politics of Jesus. Radical for me then meant going to Ireland to live the rest of my life. Radical was looking for a way to serve, which ended up being Ireland. This was when daily bombs and bomb threats were the only news we heard from there—too long ago for some of us to remember—and definitely superseded by September 11, when terrorism came to American shores. It was in the days when the "Irish conflict" was the terrorist news; it was when the IRA was the group you thought of when you heard the word *terrorist*. That was when Mennonites in London called for a group of people to come and live out the gospel of peace in Ireland, to witness from a peace church base—and help Irish people who were working at reconciliation between Catholics and Protestants.

It was a hard job. Reconciliation was not considered possible by most people in Ireland in the 1980s. So my commitment to peace in Ireland, working in groups that promoted nonviolence, pushed my radical attachment to Jesus deeper. I needed to understand where Jesus got the courage for his life, how he "for the sake of the joy that was set before him, endured the cross." I started a spiritual search and one day on a retreat—I was actually doing lectio divina with the Scripture in John 20—I was grasped by the story of Jesus appearing to his disciple Mary after his resurrection. He calls her name and she recognizes him and knows he's alive. In that encounter between Mary and Jesus so long ago, I somehow heard him call me now. I'd been a Christian for eleven years, but this was a call to me very personally—not to a group, not to a community, not even to a mission. It was a call to me as "Dawn." He used my name. He offered a call from Person to person, a call to a relationship, an invitation to deep friendship, deep knowing, deep trust.

This is a relationship of attachment that not only asks us to follow but also allows us to participate in the same power, the same love, the same life, that Jesus lived. David Augsburger puts it like this: "We are co-travelers with Christ, co-buried, co-united, co-crucified; we have co-died and now we co-live, co-inherit, co-suffer as we are co-glorified and co-formed into the Son-of-God image to become sisters and brothers with Christ" (38).

Eugene Petersen says it this way in his translation (*The Message*) of Romans 8:29-30:

God knew what he was doing from the very beginning. He decided from the outset to shape the lives of those who love him along the same lines as the life of his Son. The Son stands first in the line of humanity he restored. *We see the original and intended shape of our lives there in him* [italics mine]. After God made that decision of what his children should be like, he followed it up by calling people by name. After he called them by name, he set them on a solid basis with himself. And then, after getting them established, he stayed with them to the end, gloriously completing what he had begun.

We saw in my grandmother's life that following Jesus does not mean we all are alike. Jesus calls us each by name. There are as many ways of following as there are names, as there are individuals. But there are some similarities. Jesus treated his enemies differently. His disciples kept wanting to call down fire on his enemies, but Jesus said no. He was despised and rejected. He was killed—went like a lamb to the slaughter. Jesus lived this way out of a deep sense of being God's Beloved. We see him at his baptism soaking up the blessing of God. We see him retreating for prayer to be with his *Abba*. These are all things we learn from him about being truly human. Can we live like that? "Come, follow me," he said to his disciples. And he still calls us.

One suggestion[71]: Take the way the spiritual formation program was developed at AMBS as a model for developing a spiritual formation program for the congregational level. Have one person—a person who is experienced in and has been trained in spiritual direction and forms of prayer, including contemplative—do the writing and development work with a group of congregational people, possibly the elders, providing the review, evaluation, and stimulation the AMBS faculty provided. The history, culture and faith of the given congregation would provide the background for the development, with the six areas identified in this chapter providing the outline for the development. The curriculum for the "Personal Spirituality" course at AMBS could also provide a model for the first round of training for congregational leaders, and then members. Three congregations could be chosen to be pilot programs.

NOTES

Introduction

1. Paul Schrag, "Virtue for the Real World," *Mennonite Weekly Review*, October 23, 2006, 4.

2. See John L. Ruth, *Forgiveness: A Legacy of the West Nickel Mines Amish School* (Scottdale, Pa: Herald Press, 2007), 44.

3. Schrag. 4.

4. Ibid.

5. Dawn Ruth Nelson, "How Do We Become Like Christ? American Mennonite Spiritual Formation Through the Lens of One Woman's Life and One Seminary, 1909-2003" (D.Min. thesis, Lancaster Lancaster Theological Seminary, 2004).

6. Bradley Siebert, "Forgiveness from the Fringe," *Mennonite Weekly Review*, October 23, 2006, 5.

7. It's interesting to me how Mennonites don't seem to be able to hear this about themselves except from outsiders like McLaren.

8. Jodi H. Beyeler, "Author Urges Anabaptist Witness," *Mennonite Weekly Review*, October 30, 2006, 1.

9. At the church where I pastor, Methacton Mennonite in Norristown, Pa., it led to a Mennonite-Lutheran dialogue for Lent with the Lutheran church down the road. They wanted to meet us and talk about why this forgiveness happened. We shared the core beliefs of each tradition and became ongoing friends.

10. Beyeler, 1.

11. Arnold Snyder, "Modern Mennonite Reality and Anabaptist Spirituality," *Conrad Grebel Review* 9.1 (Winter 1991): 49.

12. Dawn Nelson, "Ireland Update," *WMSC Voice*, November 1984, 5.

13. I was so angry I went back and told the president of the seminary I had graduated from that he needed two tracks—one for men and one for women. He didn't understand and looked aghast. I

should have explained that I suggested this because the track I took was geared totally to the shape of men's lives, not to the realities—and joys—of my life as a new mother; it was not geared to the traditional shape women's lives were supposed to take in Ireland in those days, and which I found myself living out.

14. Susan Classen's little booklet published by Mennonite Central Committee, *Freely Give, Freely Receive,* describes her life as a Mennonite Central Committee worker in the violent contexts of El Salvador and Nicaragua as she drew on the resources of both the Catholic sisters she worked among and her own Mennonite tradition and heritage. Eventually Susan became the director of a Catholic retreat center where she had received spiritual direction during her years of service in Central America.

15. Tilden Edwards, *Spiritual Friend* (Mahwah, N.J.: Paulist Press, 1980), 235.

Chapter One

1. Twentieth-century American Mennonite spirituality with Swiss-German roots.

2. As I said, she died at age ninety-five in February 2005 and husband Henry died at age 101 in February 2006.

3. All quotes in the rest of this chapter are from interviews with Susan Ruth taped and transcribed by Dawn Ruth Nelson between October 2001 and October 2002.

4. My daughter Sarah Nelson's college essay.

5. Jay Ruth, *Looking at Lower Salford* (Souderton, Pa.: Indian Valley Printing Company, 1984), 144.

6. Many times I have heard from family members of Susan's mother's generosity, too. She kept a record of the many tramps who came through their area, and what she fed them.

7. Joel Alderfer, *Peace Be Unto This House: A History of The Salford Mennonite Congregation 1717-1988* (Harleysville, Pa.: Salford Mennonite Church, 1988), 52, 57.

8. J. C. Wenger, "Prayer Veiling," in the *Mennonite Encyclopedia*, ed. Harold S. Bender, Cornelius Krahn, C. Henry Smith, vol. 4, (Scottdale, Pa.: Mennonite Publishing House, 1959), 213, says this about the prayer veiling:

> Prayer Veiling, also known as the devotional covering or worship veil, is worn in worship and prayer services by the women members of certain American Mennonite bodies, and formerly by most Mennonites of Europe as well. Indeed the principle that women should worship with veiled heads can be called a historic Christian practice. [Notice the word *practice*.] . . . . The biblical basis for the worship veil is I Cor. 11: 2-16 . . . the apostle . . . begins by commending the Christians of Corinth for obediently following his instructions. . . . He then expounds the order of creation as to the

headship of man; he likens this relationship of equal persons, the one of whom is to serve as 'head', to the relationship which obtains between God and Christ (Paul does not make a four-level hierarchy; God, Christ, man, woman; he simply makes an illuminating comparison to clarify the meaning of man's headship) . . . . .In modern times the prayer veiling in the Mennonite (MC) and related groups has become a small light cap made of a fine organdy or similar material, usually white in color, but sometimes black. The form of the veil in the past 150 years in American has always been that of a cap, not a true veil, formerly almost always tied with strings. The strings are now seldom used except in the most conservative sections, and the cap is usually pinned lightly to the hair.

9. Phone conversation with Henry Ruth, June 24, 2003.

10. John Ruth e-mail, May 14, 2003.

11. Alderfer, 57.

12. John Ruth e-mail, May 14, 2003.

13. Barbara Shisler e-mail, March 3, 2002.

14. She used the King James Version here, so I left it like that.

Chapter Two

1. Thank you to Mary Jane Hershey for suggesting this sense of place as an organizing principle.

2. A quote in the book *Migrant Muses: Mennonites Writing in the U.S.*, ed. Ervin Beck and John D. Roth (Goshen, Ind.: Mennonite Historical Society, 1998), 12, says that "displacement—migration between cultures through physical dislocation as refugees, immigrants, migrants, exiles or expatriates. . . . is . . . one of the most formative experiences of our century".

3. Robert Wuthnow, "The Changing Character of American Spirituality," in *The Dilemma of Anabaptist Piety*, ed. Stephen Longenecker (Bridgewater, Va.: Penobscot Press, 1997), 110.

4. "Modern Mennonites are feeling more alienated again, and having to find the resources in the early Anabaptist texts that sound more like 'This world is not my home.'" (Anne Thayer e-mail, Feb. 12, 2003)

5. Thank you to Paul Nelson for reminding me of this idea, which I think was also stated by Reinhold Niebuhr, see John L. Ruth, *Forgiveness* (Scottdale, Pa.: Herald Press, 2007), 56.

6. Delbert Wiens, "From the Village to the City: A Grammar for the Languages We Are," *Direction* (Oct. 1973-Jan. 1974): 103

7. Dennis Martin, "Spiritual Life or Spirituality," *Mennonite Encyclopedia*, vol. 5, 851.

8. Marcus Smucker, "A Rationale for Spiritual Guidance," 7.

9. See Margaret Guenther, *At Home in the World: A Rule of Life for the Rest of Us* (New York: Seabury Books, 2006).

10. Tom Finger, abstract of paper, "How Sacramental Were the

Original Anabaptists?" (2003 conference), www.hillsdale.edu/academics/Soc/ritual.htm

11. Arvilla Bechtel, *A Medley of Memories* (Morgantown, Pa.: Masthof Press, 2001), 152-194.

12. Ibid., 100.

13. Ibid., 202.

14. Thank you to Betsy Dintaman for this idea.

15. Delbert Wiens, 103-4.

16. Ibid.

17. I am using the version of the Bible she used in this quote.

18. Bechtel, 267.

19. Marlene Kropf and Ken Nafziger, *Singing: A Mennonite Voice* (Scottdale, Pa.: Herald Press, 2001).

20. Pietism was a religious movement at the end of the seventeenth century which emphasized a heartfelt religion; "Pietism," *Mennonite Encyclopedia*, vol 4, 176. I included much more about the relation of Pietism to Mennonites in chapter 2, Nelson thesis.

21. Mary Lou Houser. *The Spirituality of Ruth Kraybill Souder: Her 103-Year Legacy 1889-1993* (Unpublished manuscript, 1997).

22. "Baptism," *The Mennonite Encyclopedia*, vol 1.

23. Quote based on Nelson thesis, 14:

Gelassenheit is a German word I will use in several chapters, and it will become even more important in the conclusion. Walter Klaassen, "Gelassenheit and Creation," *Conrad Grebel Review* 9.1 (Winter 1991): 23, says that this was a concept borrowed from medieval mystics, by sixteenth-century South German and Austrian Anabaptists. A scholar named Robert Friedmann, according to Klaassen, 23, "first reacquainted Mennonites with the mystic concept. He found it in the writings of South German and Austrian Anabaptists and discovered that it described a very important part of [these Anabaptists'] concept of the Christian life, especially their relationship to God." In the *Mennonite Encyclopedia*, volume 3, Friedmann defines gelassenheit as "self-surrender, resignation in God's will, yieldedness to God's will, self-abandonment, the (passive) opening to God's willing, including the readiness to suffer for the sake of God, also peace and calmness of mind, in Dutch devotional literature" (448). What strikes me is that the term has continued to be used through all four centuries of the Anabaptist/Mennonite tradition, up until the present time, and might therefore be fruitful and central in the future.

24. John L. Ruth, *Forgiveness*, 93.

25. "Giving-up-ness," Ibid., 93.

26. Ibid., 95.

27. Marcus Smucker, "Mennonite Spirituality," *AMBS Bulletin* 50.2 (1986).

28. Marcus Smucker, "Prayer," *Mennnonite Encyclopedia*, vol. 5, 850.

29. From self-published collection of Henry G. Gottshall (Souderton, Pa.: 1948); hymn words by Elizabeth Barrett Browning, music by Henry G. Gottshall.

30. J. Howard Kauffman and Leo Driedger, *The Mennonite Mosaic: Identity and Modernization* (Scottdale, Pa.: Herald Press, 1991), 270.

31. Kimberly Schmidt, Diane Zimmerman Umble, and Steve Reschly, eds. *Strangers at Home: Amish and Mennonite Women in History* (Baltimore, Md.: The Johns Hopkins University Press, 2002), 73.

32. Alderfer, 7.

33. Beulah S. Hostetler, Ph.D. dissertation, 269

34. Ibid., 177-178.

35. Schmidt, Umble, Reschly, 66.

36. It may also be tied to modesty and thus is more related to covering up a developing girl's shape at the time that becomes necessary.

37. Julie Musselman, "From Anna Baptist and Menno Barbie to Anna Beautiful." *Conrad Grebel Review* 16.3 (Fall 1998): 2.

38. Ibid., 9.

39. Kauffman and Driedger, 119.

40. Schmidt, Umble, Reschly, 110.

41. Bechtel, 200.

42. The German language did not reinforce separation from evil in Europe, however, where early Mennonites spoke the same language as others, so it is not necessary to speak a different language from the mainstream culture in order to be Mennonite.

43. The complete text of the Schleitheim Confession can be found online at *Global Anabaptist Mennonite Encyclopedia* online, www.gameo.org

44. Hostetler, 58-9.

45. Ibid., 57.

46. *Confession of Faith in a Mennonite Perspective* (Scottdale, Pa.: Herald Press, 1995).

47. Tieleman Jansz Van Braght, *The Martyr's Mirror* (Scottdale, Pa.: Herald Press, 1950). More information on *The Martyr's Mirror* also online at www.gameo.org

48. During war-times the book has strengthened Mennonites—by citing many previous examples beginning with Jesus and the first martyr Stephen—to follow through with their conscientious objection to war, the expression of their nonresistant convictions, when the possibility of persecution from those who misunderstand or disagree with this non-participation in war always looms.

49. Marcus Smucker, *Self-Sacrifice and Self-Realization* (Ph.D. dissertation, The Union Institute and University, 1987).

50. Ibid.

51. Ibid., 186.

Chapter Three

1. Robert Wuthnow, *After Heaven: Spirituality in America Since the 1950s* (Berkeley, Calif.: University of California Press, 1998), 6-7.

2. Ibid.

3. Beulah S. Hostetler, Ph.D. dissertation, 1.

4. Howard Kauffman and Leo Driedger, *The Mennonite Mosaic: Identity and Modernization*, (Scottdale, Pa.: Herald Press, 1991).

5. Schmidt, Umble, Reschly, 340.

6. Dorothy C. Bass, *Practicing Our Faith: A Way of Life for a Searching People* (San Francisco: Jossey-Bass Publishers, 1997), 1-2.

7. The retreats are sponsored by a program with Mennonite roots called the Kairos School of Spiritual Formation. It meets at a Jesuit Spiritual Center in Wernersville, Pa. See www.on-the-journey.org

8. In my 2004 thesis, I devoted a whole chapter to describing the phenomenon of the spiritual Dark Night and how that could describe the current sociological and soul context of Christians in America.

9. George A. Maloney S.J., *Prayer of the Heart* (Notre Dame, Ind.: Ave Maria Press, 1981), 23.

10. Ibid., 76.

11. Ibid.

12. Ibid., 81.

13. Ibid., 82.

14. Henri Nouwen, *Reaching Out: The Three Movements of the Spiritual Life* (Garden City, N.Y.: Doubelday Company, Inc. 1975), 22.

15. Dawn Ruth Nelson, "Mennonites and Cistercians in Ireland," *Gospel Herald*, December 9, 1980, 996-997.

16. See the literature review chapter of my 2004 thesis for some of the scholarly sources that explore links between sixteenth-century Mennonites and Catholic orders. Some of the authors are in the bibliography here: C. Arnold Snyder, C. J. Dyck, Dennis Martin.

17. Eoin De Bhaldraithe, "All Who Take the Sword: The Pope on Violence," *Doctrine and Life* (1980), www.dominicanpublications.com

18. Salford Mennonite Church, Harleysville, Pa.

19. John Koenig,. *New Testament Hospitality: Partnership with Strangers as Promise and Mission* (Philadelphia Pa.: Fortress Press, 1985.)

20. This was in 1980, when unemployment was high in Ireland and young people were leaving to find jobs elsewhere—before the "Celtic Tiger" economy prior to more recession.

21. See "mission as pilgrimage" in Teresa Clements D.M.J., *Missionary Spirituality: For the Praise of His Glory* (Dublin, Ireland: Carmelite Centre of Spirituality, 1987).

22. Bro. Eoin has also described meeting us in the Dublin Mennonite Community in an essay in *Coming Home: Stories of Anabaptists in Britain and Ireland*, ed. Alan Kreider and Stuart Murray (Kitchener, Ont.: Pandora Press, 2000).

Chapter 4

1. I read this statistic four years after I finished my thesis. But I added it for the book. It is from Jim Schrag's "A Study of Mennonites" in *Equipping: A Resource Packet for Equipping Mennonite Church USA Pastors and Leaders* (Newton, Kan.: Mennonite Church USA Communications Offices, January 2007). These statistics are derived from the much larger study of current Mennonite demographics by Conrad Kanagy.

2. From conversation with my spiritual director, Renee Crauder, a Quaker

3. Sandra Schneiders I.H.M., *Finding the Treasure: Locating Catholic Religious Life in a New Ecclesial and Cultural Contex*, Religious Life in a New Millenium, vol. 1 (New York/Mahwah, N. J.: Paulist Press, 2000), 183.

4. Wuthnow describes two types of spirituality in *After Heaven: Spirituality in America since the 1950s:*

> At one time, people were residents of their communities; now they are commuters. . . . The same is true of spirituality. At one time, people identified their faith by membership; now they do so increasingly by the search for various organizations, groups, and disciplines, all the while feeling marginal to any particular group or place. (6-7)

Courtney Bender, in an essay called "Place, Process and Practice: Perspectives on Changes in the Character of Mennonite Spirituality," in Longenecker, 126-127, questions some of Wuthnow's analysis:

> It bears noting that scholars of American religious history continue to pile up studies documenting the presence and strength of extra-doxic, extra-institutional spiritual activity among Catholics and Protestants of every stripe. The same is true of Mennonites. In the past, normal church-going Mennonites visited faith healers, went to camp meetings, used white magic and zodiacal almanacs, and put hex signs on their barns. Religious authority varyingly sanctioned, controlled, rejected, or ignored such practices. While Mennonites were certainly more rooted to a place, church, and community than many of us are now, the forms of spirituality that they found meaningful and useful were not necessarily those practiced in churches.

Bender observes, however, that

> Mennonites do not seem to replace standard Christian spiritual practices with alternative spiritual practices. For, despite all of the other changes in beliefs and values documented in the *Mennonite Mosaic*, its authors find that the percentage of individuals continuing standard Christian devotional practices, including prayer, Bible reading, feeling close to God, and asking God for guidance, remained constant.

5. We also need a more explicit, open-and-understandable-to-oth-

ers biblical Anabaptist-Mennonite statement of theology; John Roth—*Beliefs: Mennonite Faith and Practice* (Scottdale, Pa.: Herald Press, 2005)—and others are doing that.

6. Marcus Smucker, "Spiritual Direction and Spiritual Formation," *Mennonite Encyclopedia*, vol. 5, 851.

7. Dennis Martin, "Spiritual Life or Spirituality," *Mennonite Encyclopedia*, vol. 5, 852.

8. Ibid.

9. Robert Wuthnow, "The Changing Character of American Spirituality," in Longenecker, 110.

10. Al Dueck, "Anabaptists, Pietism and the Therapeutic Culture," in Longenecker, 162

11. A degree called Master of Arts in Spiritual Formation is offered at AMBS. There is also a program of spiritual formation offered at Eastern Mennonite Seminary in Harrisonburg, Virginia, which I did not have time to fully research although I was in touch with two of the professors in that program, Wendy Miller and John Martin—this will be a research job for someone else!

Chapter Five

1. *Confession of Faith in a Mennonite Perspective* (Scottdale, Pa.: Herald Press, 1995), 69.

2. Urban T. Holmes III, *A History of Christian Spirituality: An Analytical Introduction* (New York: The Seabury Press, 1980).

3. Holmes, *A History of Christian Spirituality*, 1.

4. Ibid., 2.

5. Ibid., 7.

6. Harold Bender, Cornelius Krahn, C. Henry Smith, eds. *The Mennonite Encyclopedia*, vols. 1-4 (Scottdale, Pa.: Mennonite Publishing House, 1955-1959).

7. Kent Groff, "Theopractice: A New Look at Spirituality" in *Drawing from the Well: Reflections for Praying, Thinking and Acting with Integrity* 1.1 (Oasis Ministries, December 2005), 3-4

8. David Augsburger, *Dissident Spirituality: A Spirituality of Self-Surrender, Love of God, and Love of Neighbor* (Grand Rapids, Mich.: Brazos Press, 2006), 15.

9. Myron Augsburger *Walking in the Resurrection.* (Scottdale, Pa.: Pa.: Herald Press, 1976), 71.

10. Marcus Smucker, "A Proposal for Spiritual Disciplines," in Nelson thesis, Appendix E, 259.

11. Marcus Smucker, "A Rationale for Spiritual Guidance in the Mennonite Church," (Unpublished essay, 2002).

12. Marcus Smucker, *Mennonite Encyclopedia*, vol. 5, 850.

13. Alisdair MacIntyre, *After Virtue: A Study in Moral Theology.* 2nd. ed. (Notre Dame, Ind.: University of Notre Dame Press, 1984), 187.

14. Wuthnow, in *After Heaven: Spirituality in America Since the 1950s*, 16, points to the concept of a "practice-based spirituality" as

the most promising way forward in a time of conflicting, confusing spiritual options. "In my view," he says,

> the ancient wisdom that emphasizes the idea of spiritual practices needs to be rediscovered [as an alternative to either dwelling-oriented or seeking-oriented spirituality]. . . . Spiritual practices put responsibility squarely on individuals to spend time on a regular basis worshipping, communing with, listening to, and attempting to understand the ultimate source of sacredness in their lives. Spiritual practices can be performed in the company of others, and they are inevitably embedded in religious institutions, but they must also be performed individually. . . . Spiritual practices require individuals to engage reflectively in a conversation with their past. . . . Spiritual practices have a moral dimension. . . . Spiritual practices have largely been ignored in recent scholarship. . . . Spiritual practice is a way of retrieving the neglected middle in our understandings of religion.

15. Dorothy C. Bass, ed. *Practicing Our Faith: A Way of Life for a Searching People* (San Francisco: Jossey-Bass Publishers, 1997), 5.

16. Sandra Schneiders, *New Wineskins: Re-Examining Religious Life Today* (New York/Mahwah: Paulist Press, 1986), 222.

17. Constance FitzGerald, OCD, "The Desire for God and the Transformative Power of Contemplation," in *Light Burdens, Heavy Blessings: Challenges of Church and Culture in the Post-Vatican II Era: Essays in Honor of Margaret Brennan*, ed. Mary Heather MacKinnon, Moni McIntyre, Mary Ellen Sheehan (Franciscan Press, 2000).

18. Often, meetings are monthly for approximately an hour.

19. William A. Barry and William J. Connolly, *The Practice of Spiritual Direction* (San Francisco: Harper Collins, 1982).

20. Ibid., 5

21. Ibid., 8

22. Walter Klaassen, "Gelassenheit and Creation," *Conrad Grebel Review* 9.1 (Winter 1991): 23.

23. Robert Friedmann. "Gelassenheit," *The Mennonite Encyclopedia*, vol. 2, 448.

24. Tilden Edwards, *Spiritual Friend* (Mahwah, N.J.: Paulist Press, 1980), 2 .

25. See Sandra Cronk, *Dark Night Journey: Inward Repatterning Toward a Life Centered in God* (Wallingford, Pa.: Pendle Hill Publications, 1991).

26. See Nelson thesis for an entire chapter (ch. 5) on the Dark Night among Mennonites.

27. Sandra Schneiders, I.H.M, *Finding the   Treasure: Locating Catholic Religious Life in a New Ecclesial and Cultural Context*, Religious Life in a New Millenium, vol. 1 (New York/Mahwah, N.J.: Paulist Press, 2000).

28. *Confession of Faith in a Mennonite Perspective*, 70 .

29. Ibid., 69.

30. In Marlene Kropf and Eddy Hall, *Praying with the Anabaptist: The Secret of Bearing Fruit* (Newton, Kan: Faith & Life Press, 1984), 29.

31. I heard this point first made by Wendy Miller, professor at Eastern Mennonite Seminary, Harrisonburg, Virginia.

32. *Confession of Faith in a Mennonite Perspective,* 69

33. From Smucker interview in Nelson thesis, Appendix A, 198-199.

34. John Roth, "Pietism and the Anabaptist Soul," in Longenecker, 33. Also see chapter 2, Nelson thesis, for a longer discussion of Roth and the perceived threat of Pietism in twentieth-century Mennonite theology.

Chapter 6

1. Interviews with Marlene Kropf and Marcus Smucker and e-mails from Thelma Groff and Erland Waltner can be found in Nelson thesis, Appendix C.

In summary, Marcus Smucker moved from growing up as an Amish child in Lancaster County to PAX service in Europe after World War II to college in Virginia, then seminary at New York Theological seminary and thence to an inner city pastorate on the West Coast. Marlene Kropf went from a childhood in a traditional rural Oregon congregation to teaching and a Mennonite Central Committee term in Jamaica that changed her forever. Marlin Miller grew up near Goshen, Indiana, then went to Japan as a college student for a year, which his wife now says began to change him, and later he served in Europe for a decade. Thelma Groff served with her husband Weyburn in India for eighteen years. In that separation from community they all experienced thirty-five to forty years ago, what many Mennonites are experiencing now, as the traditional community and spiritual formation structures are dying, along with the people who can still remember growing up in them and who were formed by them.

2. I became increasingly aware as I wrote this that there would be many other important stories to follow, such as the story of Gene and Mary Herr, who have been so influential in the realm of spirituality in the Mennonite church and who eventually started a retreat center in Three Rivers, Michigan. I just had to decide to limit the study in some way, so I focused on what happened at AMBS and the key players there. Someone else will have to look more in depth at the history of what the Herrs did.

3. Jim Lapp also mentioned that he had Mary and Gene to his Albany, Oregon, congregation in the 1970s and subsequently he and his wife Nancy started going to monasteries once a month, conversation Sept. 26, 2002.

4. Kropf interview in Nelson thesis, Appendix B, 200-201.

5. Goshen Biblical Seminary was one of two seminaries that jointly operated at Elkhart and eventually merged into Associated Mennonite Biblical Seminaries, then more recently Associated Mennonite Biblical Seminary.

6. John Howard Yoder, *The Politics of Jesus*, 2nd. ed. (Grand Rapids, Mich.: Eerdmans, 1994).

7. "Pietistic" was the other bad label thrown around frequently. I began to understand why after reviewing some recent literature on Mennonite scholar Robert Friedmann in the 1940s and his thesis on the threat of Pietism to Anabaptism. I discuss this much more in-depth in the review of writings on Mennonite spirituality,Nelson thesis, chapter 2.

8. Thelma Groff is an interesting person in her own right. She lived in India from 1946-1964, sent by the Mennonite Board of Missions. She supplied the following information about her perspective and experience. I asked her how she got interested in spirituality concerns. She replied:

> I joined a small group at College Mennonite Church led by Gene and Mary Herr. Together we studied "Fire in Coventry." They spoke highly of a week spent at Church of the Savior Retreat Center in MD called Dayspring. So we [husband Weyburn Groff and I] went. It was our first experience of a week-long retreat in silence and we were blessed. At the same time as all of this was happening I became aware of the Ira Progroff Journal Writing training sessions and I completed the three levels. I also sought out a spiritual director and found helpful women through my visits for retreat to Mary's Solitude at Notre Dame in South Bend.
>
> One summer I spent two weeks at Bloomfield Hills near Detroit as a participant in workshops on prayer. When Herrs moved to Elkhart they put out a call for persons who wanted to give themselves to the establishing of a place of prayer in this area. We joined them and others in a group which was structured after the pattern lived out in Church of the Savior. During this time Weyburn and I were asked to lead silent retreats at a number of Mennonite church camps. This included Friday night through Sunday noon retreats in congregations. We were involved in this ministry from the early '70s through mid-'80s.
>
> During Weyburn's first sabbatical spent pastoring at Albany, Oregon, I found a congregational pastor teaching a course on Spiritual Direction at a Monastery. AMBS gave me credit for that and gradually then I began responding to requests for spiritual direction. Interest within the denomination was growing so after leading a workshop at the General Assembly at Ames, Iowa, *I then called, as far as I know, the first gathering of Mennonite Spiritual Directors at General Assembly at Purdue* [italics mine] It was very informal and didn't last more than an hour. About twenty people attended. We wrestled among other things with "who am I to call

myself a spiritual director?" A spirituality committee composed of persons from across the denomination was formed and this was helpful.

[As far as the beginnings of the program at AMBS] I remember being very moved by a speaker from a seminary in Europe who told AMBS faculty that he had found few "prayers" in his seminary community. Others amongst us were also moved. The time to be more intentional on campus about spiritual growth had come. I was asked to give ¼ time at AMBS. *The [AMBS] faculty sent me to a month long Ignatian Silent Retreat held at a Retreat Center just north of Cincinnati.* To experience the value of that was so convincing that I kept trying (unsuccessfully) to have something similar become a requirement at AMBS.

To help us get in touch with where students were, Marcus and I worked out the following questionnaire:—1) Describe your experience of God. 2) What do you desire from your experience of God? 3) How do you nurture your experience with God? 4) In what ways does your experience of God affect your experience of yourself? 5) In what ways does your experience of God influence your relationship with others? 6) How is your seminary experience helping/hindering your experience of God, self and others? This was a good set of questions, but exactly how we used them I don't recall. I imagine they guided us as we met individually with students.

We offered and led a weekly early morning (pre classes) prayer group in the chapel. There we practiced Centering Prayer: in silence learning how to quiet our minds and pay loving attention to God. We made lectionary readings available in the prayer room. I remember using "guided imagery," praying the scripture, reflective journaling and silence with various groups (even faculty and the AMBS Board members) and in chapels occasionally. We took students on retreats. We gave spiritual direction to a few who requested it. . . . We encouraged them to go on private retreats—to the Hermitage, [to] St. Mary's or [to] the upstairs of our house on 8th. Street [Goshen] known as the Upper Room.

God has been good to bless and expand these offerings at AMBS. It is particularly exciting to me that students are being supervised and enabled to become spiritual directors and that intentional spiritual growth is happening throughout our denomination. e-mail from Thelma Groff to Dawn Nelson, January 3, 2003.

Yesterday I found the following quote from [Erland Waltner] in his letter to me upon my retirement: "We think of you as one of the true pioneers in the new emphasis on spirituality at AMBS." e-mail from Thelma Groff to Dawn Nelson, January 14, 2003

9. See interviews in Nelson thesis, Appendixes A, B.

10. I also learned recently from talking to Marlin's widow Ruthann Miller that a year in Japan as a college student was very

important for Marlin. They weren't married yet at that point but she knew him well. She said that year in Japan he began to rethink his faith.

11. Marlin also served as a consultant for MBM program in West Africa and did part-time postgraduate study in Paris. He was Mennonite Central Committee's European Peace Section representative. During the period 1963-75, Marlin participated in the Puidoux conferences on church and state, and was involved in various East-West conversations and travel in the GDR and Czechslovakia. He was president of Eirene International Service for Peace from 1970 to 1974

12. Information from Barbara Nelson-Gingerich e-mail, Nov. 13, 2002.

13. All subsequent interview quotes are from my interview with Marcus Smucker on January 13, 2002 in Appendix A, Nelson thesis.

14. Ibid., 188

15. Ibid., 189.

16. Interview with Marlene Kropf, May 2, 2002, appears in full in Nelson thesis, Appendix B.

17. Ibid., 219.

18. Marlin Miller, "A Genuine Biblical Spirituality," *Gospel Herald,* Aug 31, 1982.

19. Ibid., 587.

20. Ibid.

21. Ibid.

22. Miller, *Gospel Herald,* 587. The article continues to say that

some voices among Mennonites and other denominations are saying that genuine Christian spirituality has to do with the believer's personal and private life *rather than* with the quality of the believer's life as it becomes publicly visible. This tendency misinterprets Jesus' teaching and example. Jesus withdrew to be alone with God and to pray particularly on occasions of important events in his public ministry. Furthermore, Jesus' words against practicing one's piety in public in Matthew 6 follow his teaching about the disciples' being like a city on a hill in Matthew 5. Jesus' followers are called to be reconciled with each other even before bringing their offerings to God, to remain faithful in marriage, to tell the truth in public as well as in private, to practice a new pattern of justice, and to show love to those considered to be enemies of one's own nation, class, profession, and kind. Such actions will be publicly visible. They are visible expressions of a new quality of life which seeks first God's kingdom and righteousness. Jesus incarnated this quality of life and called his disciples to do the same. It is a spirituality which expresses itself in *both* private prayer *and* public practice without playing one off against the other.

23. Kropf interview in Nelson thesis, 213.

24. Weyburn's e-mail comments to Dawn Nelson:

Thelma asked me to respond a bit to your paper from the perspective of time prior to Marcus and Marlene's coming to the seminary. There had been the coming together of the two seminaries in 1959 and then the social upheaval of the '60s and the Vietnam War. Waves reverberated through the seminary community that brought significant changes. Some time in all of this a two year curriculum review process called The Dean's Seminar examined carefully what shape the seminary curriculum should take based on the theology and mission of the Mennonite Churches. A report of this study was written by Dean Ross Bender in *The People of God: In a Believers' Church Perspective. I think the distinctive spiritual formation style would have been identified as "communal"* (italics mine).

In addition, one should note that "K-groups" (interactive fellowship and personal sharing) were designed (including faculty, students, staff and spouses) to foster spiritual growth and development supplementing academic work. Each semester there were pastors, missionaries, other church leaders invited to campus under the rubric of Theological Center guests. Each shared by public presentations and individual sharing for a period of two or three weeks. A significant visitor as far as spiritual life and prayer was concerned was Charles Whiston (some time in the '70s). He was a retired professor from Pacific Theological Seminary who was visiting (on invitation) many seminaries speaking about the importance of prayer. He also conducted special retreats for faculty. Some AMBS faculty participated in one at Yokefellow Institute (Richmond, Ind.) in 1964.

Another important ten-day retreat for some faculty (1968, 1969) was at Institute for Advanced Pastoral Study in Bloomfield Hills, Mich. These were led by Reuel Howe and staff and composed by design of ten pastors, and ten seminary faculty persons from many denominations. Another special seminar attended by some students and faculty persons was led by Tilden Edwards from Wellspring Retreat Center in Washington. This focused on spiritual growth and provision for it in seminary. Dawn, I offer this background history to show that many streams flowed toward the development of the present *spiritual formation* program. [italics mine]

25. E-mail to Dawn Nelson from C. J. Dyck, Nov. 19, 2002.

26. Quote from Erland Waltner e-mail to Dawn Nelson, Jan. 20, 2003, regarding what C. J. Dyck said about not remembering Marlin Miller talking about a need for a spirituality focus:

Thanks for sharing the e-mail response you got from C. J. Dyck on your Spirituality Curriculum project. I still believe that Marlin Miller did encourage Marcus Smucker to work at developing a Spiritual Disciplines Curriculum though I do not have immediate documentary evidence for this. C. J. Dyck, as a historian, tended to work with Spiritual Disciplines from a historical descriptive perspective. *What Marlin and then Marcus were deeply interested in was practical application in the lives of students and graduates. Thus the Spiritual Disciplines Curriculum got moved from the Theology and History Department to the Work of the Church Department, where it still functions.* [italics mine] . . . one can teach Spiritual Disciplines historically and Dyck, Pipkin, and later Karl Koop did, or one can teach them pastorally, as Marcus and Marlene and some others here have done. Both approaches are valid but serve different functions. AMBS has offered both kinds of courses.

27. Gayle Gerber Koontz, "RE: research project," e-mail to Dawn Nelson, Oct. 24, 2002.

28. Jacob Elias e-mail to Dawn Nelson, October 24, 2002.

29. Quoted in an e-mail from Thelma Groff, Jan. 14, 2003.

30. Kropf interview in Nelson thesis, Appendix B, 216.

31. Ibid.

32. Ibid.

33. These comments by Marlene Kropf continue below. The interview in full is in Nelson thesis, but here are a few more interesting quotes: In fact, Marlene noticed that Canadian Mennonite seminary students came to her for spiritual direction more than U. S. students, as she began offering direction at the seminary.

She began to wonder why. As she talked to the Canadian students, she discovered that they wanted to learn to pray. They remembered their grandparents praying in ways that demonstrated a strong connection to God, and they felt something lacking in their own connection to God, as they studied to be pastors. When they talked about wanting to learn to pray, Kropf would ask them, "Well, how do you pray?" They would answer: "Well, I really don't pray very much. I pray when I go to church (the communal structure). . . . my parents went to church. They did all the right things, but I didn't see that same warm faith in my parents that I saw in my grandparents."

Their grandparents were Russian Mennonites who emigrated to Canada and went through "fire and hell to get here and their faith was forged in persecution and in death and famine, and if you don't have your own connection to God, you don't have anything in that kind of story," Kropf reminded me in her interview. "Those grandparents came [from terrible situations in Russia] and eked out a living on the prairies. . . . [But] their children became well-to-do and invested so much energy in becoming assimilated into the new culture and getting wealthy . . . that they lived off [the previous generation's faith]."

Kropf is very aware that this is "a huge generalization, and a bit stern" but her experience with Canadian Mennonite seminary students in the 1980s and 1990s is helpful in analyzing why a shift is taking place now, as she observes that the parents didn't have the same depth of faith that their parents had, because they hadn't needed God in the same way. They hadn't had that terrible life in which you're thrown only on God's mercy. Were they Christian? Yes. Were they Mennonite? Yes. They would have adhered to the [Mennonite] Confession of Faith jot and tittle. But what they passed on to their children was lacking. And it was their grandchildren. . . . Those were the ones who were coming to me. . . . The grandchildren came to a seminary where they saw something else being taught. They saw another kind of praying, another kind of way of relating to Scripture and they looked at their own lives, and said, "I know what this looks like—I saw it in my grandparents but I don't have it in myself, and maybe spiritual direction is a way to get it."

And what I would ask myself then was, And if there isn't an intervention in the grandchildren's generation, what happens to their children? And I think their children become good moral secular people. I think that's how quickly you lose that warm personal faith if it isn't cultivated by adversity or cultivated intentionally in community. Of course, the grandchildren had gone to the city. They were no longer embedded in the old communities. So I saw that what we were doing at AMBS was not bringing in something new but sort of fanning the flame that was still there but was burning low because the churches hadn't taught in explicit ways what you do with the Bible, how you pray, how you listen, how you hear something. That hadn't been necessary to teach when you had this strong communal thing, and the grandparents just somehow passed that on to their grandchildren. I think it got passed on in everyday, ordinary ways. But when you don't have that, then you have to have the structures. That's how I think of spiritual direction—as a structure that makes up for something that was there instinctively before. Kropf Interview, 217

The "everyday, ordinary ways" the faith got passed on instinctively—this is what I was trying to find in my grandmother's life. And spiritual direction as a structure that makes up for what was there instinctively is the way the seminary went and the way I went in Ireland. I also notice that it was in the 1970s, which for many Mennonites was one generation off the farm, that the concern for "spirituality" erupted.

34. I also phototocopied in the thesis some of the spirituality syllabi and proposals that were produced in the 1980s and 1990s, in Appendixes D, E.

35. Smucker interview, Nelson thesis, 194.

36. Ibid., 195.

37. Kropf interview, Nelson thesis, 221.

38. Ibid., 215.

39. Thelma Groff and Marcus Smucker, "Spirituality Concerns: A Tentative Proposal for the School Year 1983-84" (Elkhart, Ind.: AMBS,

unpublished document in the AMBS Archives).

40. Ibid., 3.

41. The 1985 Proposal can be read in full in Nelson thesis, the Appendix E.

42. Smucker Proposal, in Nelson thesis, 246.

43. Ibid., 247.

44. Ibid., 248.

45. Ibid., 248.

46. At my grandmother's church, Salford Mennonite, as recently as the 1970s and 1980s, discipline was practiced the old way—specific confessions in church services on Sunday morning. I will quote from a history book, since I was not a member of this church at that time, and my grandmother also gave one or two examples of this kind of discipline in her story (discipline for singing in quartets).

> [In 1971] at the spring "council meeting" the week before communion, we experienced an outpouring of emotional and spiritual expression. There was no sermon that morning, but minister "Willie" Miller opened the service for testimonies and sharing. Person after person came forward for about two hours to share burdens, testimonies, and confessions. There were many tears that morning. . . . Alderfer, 70

In another example, Joel Alderfer, 73, tells of when

> in one memorable Sunday morning service in 1982 the issue of divorce and remarriage came to a crisis point in the congregation. A number of congregational meetings on the issue followed. The couple involved, who were seeking to be remarried with the consent of the congregation, made an emotional confession and statement of their situation in front of the whole congregation, asking forgiveness. Many persons from the congregation responded to the couple, offering support and counsel, in a session that lasted an hour or more. The congregation eventually gave this couple its consent and support on their remarriage. The same basic process occurred several times over the next couple of years, with other couples seeking remarriage. Each situation was handled individually, with great concern and a number of congregational meetings. There was little 'streamlining' of the process after it had first been done. These meetings demonstrated to the congregation and to visitors that our church does not take such issues lightly, but with much communication and discernment among the members.

It could be that Salford was one of the last congregations to still be doing it the old way. Now it has even ceased in this congregation. Something like what is described above did not happen when I attended there 1991-2003.

47. Smucker Proposal, in Nelson thesis, 259.

48. Ibid.
49. Ibid., 255.
50. Ibid., 254.

Chapter Seven

1. Delbert Wiens, "From the Village to the City: A Grammar for the Languages We Are,"*Direction* (Oct. 1973-Jan. 1974), 103-104.

2. A phrase from an interesting chapter of a book by then-graduate student Courtney Bender called "Place, Processs, and Practice: Perspectives on Changes in the Character of Mennonite Spirituality," in Longenecker.

3. Wuthnow, "The Changing Character of American Spirituality," in Longenecker, 120, says,

> I want to. . . . [raise] a normative question and [pose] a tentative answer. The normative question is how people of faith, living in the unsettled times that characterize our society, can deepen their faith, if they choose to do so, rather than adopting a spiritual style that merely imitates the consumerist, fast food orientation of the wider culture, and that in many cases results in such a fragmented, do-it-yourself spirituality that its practitioners appear to be flaky rather than trustworthy or sincere? The answer to which I want to point briefly may lie in the ancient wisdom of devotional practices. That is, spirituality may indeed have to be pieced together from many different sources for it to satisfy our increasingly diverse identities, but it can be pieced together reflectively, deliberately [that is what I try to do in this book, and what I believe AMBS did] if its practitioners make conscious efforts to reflect on their spirituality, to learn from but also to set aside the influences of the spiritual marketplace, and in the process to pray . . . commemorating the past as they deliberate about its meanings for the future.

4. Wiens, 103-4.

5. E-mail from John Ruth, Feb. 17, 2003.

6. This is from my interview with Marlene Kropf. This quote is in a note in Nelson thesis, chapter 6.

7. Marlene Kropf interview, Nelson thesis, 215.

8. See the literature review (1980-2003) in chapter 2, Nelson thesis.

9. The syllabus is described briefly in Nelson thesis, 147-148.

10. It was also a reaction to the "legalism" of the first half of the twentieth-century Mennonite church. (See Smucker's Proposal, Nelson thesis, Appendix E), and there will perhaps soon be a swing back to more outward forms again. The children who grew up since that "legalism" ended will be looking for something, perhaps the "New Monasticism" called for in Jonathan R. Wilson, *Living Faithfully in a Fragmented World: Lessons for the Church from MacIntyre's After Virtue* (Harrisburg, Pa.: Trinity Press International, 1997).

11. *Confession of Faith in a Mennonite Perspective.*

12. Marcus Smucker's Proposal, Nelson thesis, Appendix E, lists these older practices: "there have been a variety of practices and expressions of piety in Mennonite life designed to help the individual and the church to be faithful 'followers of Jesus,' e.g., patterns of dress, simplicity of life, honesty, truthfulness, returning good for evil, regular bible reading and prayer—all to help us live the Godly life." Smucker also mentions "excommunication, baptism, communion, church rules, function of the Deacons, sermons of exhortation" (248).

13. Tom Finger, Abstract of paper for a conference in 2003 called "How Sacramental were the Original Anabaptists?" Conference, (Hillsdale College, 2003), www.hillsdale.edu/academics/Soc/ritual.htm

14. Marlin Miller, "Biblical Spirituality," *Gospel Herald,* Aug. 31, 1982, 587.

15. Dawn Ruth Nelson, *Finding God on Broad Street* (sermon 1994) and Margaret Hebblethwaite, *Motherhood and God* (London: Geoffrey Chapman, 1984).

16. Nuns and priests who have abandoned the wearing of a habit still have standards of modesty and simplicity that might be a model for Mennonites. I am not suggesting Mennonites should dress like nuns, but nuns could provide us a model of how not to throw the baby out with the bathwater.

17. Marlene Kropf and Hall, Eddy. *Praying with the Anabaptists: The Secret of Bearing Fruit* (Newton, Kan.: Faith and Life Press, 1984).

18. Dennis Linn, Sheila Fabricant Linn, and Matthew Linn, *Sleeping with Bread: Holding What Gives You Life* (Mahwah, N.J.: Paulist Press, 1995).

19. James Stewart Crawford, "Ignatian Spirituality and the Reformed Tradition." (D.Min. thesis, Lancaster Theological Seminary, 2007).

20. Kent Groff, *Active Spirituality: A Guide for Seekers and Ministers* (Herndon, Va.: The Alban Institute, 1993).

21. Tilden Edwards, *Spiritual Friend* (Mahwah, N.J.: Paulist Press, 1980).

22. Jane Hoober Peiffer and John Stahl-Wert, *Welcoming New Christians: A Guide for the Christian Initiation of Adults* (Newton, Kan.: Faith and Life Press, 1995), 12.

23. Material simplicity is also important but less often mentioned is the inner aspect of simplicity, so I have focussed on that.

24. Dietrich Bonhoeffer, *Life Together: The Classic Exploration of Faith in Community* (San Francisco: Harper San Francisco, 2003).

25. Henri Nouwen, "Solitude: The Inner Fabric of Christian Community," *Sojourners,* March 1979.

26. I have been experimenting with this at my church, Methacton Mennonite, with an occasional Sunday afternoon event called "Silent Sundays at Methacton."

27. Avery Brook, *Hidden in Plain Sight: The Practice of Christian Meditation* (Nashville, Tenn.: The Upper Room, 1978), 22.

28. Dorothy C. Bass, ed. *Practicing Our Faith: A Way of Life for a Searching People* (San Francisco: Jossey-Bass Publishers, 1997), 52-53.
29. Ibid., 55.
30. Richard Foster, *Celebration of Discipline: The Path to Spiritual Growth*, 20th. Anniversary ed. (San Francisco: Harper, 1998), 13.
31. For example, Ronald J. Sider, *The Scandal of the Evangelical Conscience: Why Are Christians Living Just Like the Rest of the World?* (Grand Rapids, Mich.: Baker Books, 2005).
32. Quoted in an editorial by Rockhill Mennonite Community (Sellersville, Pa.) CEO, Ron Sawatsky, in their community magazine, *Horizons*, Spring 2003.
33. David Augsburger, *Dissident Spirituality: A Spirituality of Self-Surrender, Love of God, and Love of Neighbor* (Grand Rapids, Mich.: Brazos Press, 2006).
34. Marcus Smucker, "A Proposal for Spiritual Disciplines at AMBS" in Nelson thesis, Appendix E, 255.
35. Marcus Smucker, "Self-Sacrifice and Self-Realization in Menno-nite Spirituality" (Ph.D. dissertation, The Union Institute and University, 1987). In Nelson thesis, 27-28, I included this synopsis of Smucker's work:

> What is interesting about Smucker's dissertation on self-sacrifice and self-realization is the way he holds together important human developmental dynamics and Anabaptist theology. It is particularly interesting because he grew up in a quintessentially Anabaptist community—in a Lancaster County Amish family, so that what he says is based on living in a real community not a theoretical one. He describes briefly what having lived in that community did to real people, that is, to himself and his family. So often in Mennonite literature, living in community is discussed and praised in the abstract.
>
> Smucker does not romanticize community as a concept divorced from the actual pains and joys of being together with other people, and he calls for the use of psychological insights to build individuals for the difficult task of being in close relationships. He discusses the need for modern Mennonites to develop ego strength as one of the tasks of Mennonite spirituality. Smucker also makes a point of calling for a "spiritual community" rather than a "spatial" one. We cannot go back to the farm and the agricultural community, as some Mennonites tried to do in the 1950s and 1960s. Smucker's "spiritual community" is perhaps related to Wuthnow's concept of a spirituality of "seeking" rather than a spirituality of "place."
>
> Smucker concludes his dissertation by formulating a "relational spirituality" based on the nature of God, who is "fundamentally relational" (Smucker, "Self-Sacrifice" 246). He distinguishes a "spirituality with a fundamentally relational foundation" from "one that is primarily mystical in orientation, although these two views are important in any spirituality". "A relational theology will tend to

highlight the quality of relationships, spiritual presence, the significance of human individuality in the I-Thou encounter, along with honesty, ethical faithfulness, intimacy and spiritual communion, service and 'suffering with' [others] in behalf of God's heartfelt concern" (246).

Based on this relational theology, Smucker concludes that self-sacrifice and self-realization can work together: "If intimate communion with a fully developed individual who yields him or herself to God's transforming presence is the goal of this relationship, then great care must be exercised to have each person, male and female, come to the greatest maturity possible in the presence of God." Maturity is reached partly through self-realization, in order to relate that self to God.

36. Joann Wolski Conn, *Spirituality and Personal Maturity* (New York: Paulist Press, 1989).

37. Beulah S. Hostetler, Ph.D. dissertation, 178.

38. Marlene Kropf, "Sisters and Brothers to Keep Us Faithful on the Way," *Gospel Herald*, April 29, 1997, and Marcus Smucker, "A Rationale for Spiritual Guidance in the Mennonite Church" (unpublished essay, 2002).

39. Professor at Eastern Mennonite Seminary, Wendy Miller's book *Learning to Listen* (Nashville, Tenn.: Upper Room Books, 1995) is helpful here.

40. Doris Janzen Longacre, *More-with-Less Cookbook* (Scottdale, Pa.: Herald Press, 1976.)

41. Conversation with Pam Landis, February 2003.

42. Gordon Houser, "Passing the Peas," *The Mennonite*, Oct. 15, 2002, 30

43. Susan Classen, *A Spirituality of Service Freely Give, Freely Receive*, MCC Occasional Paper 29 (Akron, Pa.: Mennonite Central Committee, January 2003).

44. *Confession of Faith in a Mennonite Perspective*, 70.

45. Ted Koontz, Syllabus from "Spirituality and Peacemaking" class (Elkhart, Ind.: Associated Mennonite Biblical Seminary).

46. Marcus Smucker, *AMBS Bulletin* 50.2 (Winter 1985): 2.

47. Arnold Snyder, "Modern Mennonite Reality and Anabaptist Spirituality: Balthasar Hubmaier's Catechism of 1526," *Conrad Grebel Review* 9.1(Winter 1991): 41.

48. Ibid., 49.

49. John R. Martin *Ventures in Discipleship* (Scottdale, Pa.: Herald Press, 1984.)

50. Walter Klaassen "Gelassenheit and Creation," *Conrad Grebel Review* 9.1 (Winter 1991): 23-36.

51. Ibid., 32

52. *Confession*, 70-71.

53. Joann Wolsky Conn, *Spirituality and Personal Maturity*; Marlene Kropf, "Female Spirituality," lecture to class on Spiritual Formation

(Lancaster, Pa.: Feb. 2002, available from author).

54. Marcus Smucker, "Self-Sacrifice and Self-Realization."

55. Marcus Smucker, "Prayer (Mennonites)," *Mennonite Encyclopedia*, vol. 5, 717.

56. Marcus Smucker, "A Rationale for Spiritual Guidance in the Mennonite Church," (Unpublished essay, 2002), 8.

57. J. Nelson Kraybill "The Center of our Hope," *AMBS Window*, Summer 2003, 1.

58. Kenneth R. Davis, *Anabaptism and Asceticism* (Scottdale, Pa.: Herald Press, 1974.)

59. Quoted in AMBS Board minutes in response to Thelma Groff and Marcus Smucker. "Spirituality Concerns: A Tentative Proposal for the School Year 1983-84" (Elkhart, Ind.: Associated Mennonite Biblical Seminary, Archives, reported in an e-mail from Rosie Reschly to Dawn Nelson, June 19, 2002).

60. See John Veltri, *Week of Directed Prayer in a Church Setting: A Manual* (available from Office of Religious Education, Diocese of Hamilton, 700 King Street West, Hamilton, Ontario L8P 1C7, Canada); or develop a set of Mennonite spiritual exercises based on John Martin's *Ventures in Discipleship*.

61. Rosemary Stutzman, ed. *Soul Care: How to Plan and Guide Inspirational Retreats* (Scottdale, Pa.: Herald Press, 2003).

62. The syllabus is in Nelson thesis, Appendix D, 242-245.

63. Marlin Miller.

64. Arnold Snyder, *Biblical Concordance of the Swiss Brethren, 1540* (Kitchener, Ont.: Pa.: Pandora Press, 2001), xvi.

65. Robin Maas and Gabriel O'Donnell, *Spiritual Traditions for the Contemporary Church* (Nashville, Tenn.: Abingdon Press, 1990), 292.

66. Marlene Kropf and Ken Nafziger, *Singing: A Mennonite Voice* (Scottdale, Pa.: Herald Press, 2001).

67. These are similar to the three "rules" in Marcus Smucker, "Rationale for Spiritual Guidance in the Mennonite Church": the rule of prayer, the rule of Christ/community; the rule of service.

68. See Marcus Smucker, "A Rationale for Spiritual Guidance in the Mennonite Church."

69. Stanley Hauerwas "Confessions of a Mennonite Camp Follower," *Mennonite Quarterly Review* 74.4 (October 2000): 24.

70. David Augsburger, *Dissident Spirituality: A Spirituality of Self-Surrender, Love of God, and Love of Neighbor* (Grand Rapids, Mich.: Brazos Press, 2006).

71. This proposal came from Lamont Woelk, a member of Salford Mennonite church, after he read my thesis. He goes on to get even more specific: "A possible option would be to have the Franconia Conference office take leadership in this, choosing three congregations with people who have an interest in spiritual formation to be the actual settings for such development"; e-mail from Lamont Woelk to Dawn Nelson, Dec. 08, 2003.

BIBLIOGRAPHY

Alderfer, Joel D. *Peace Be Unto This House: A History of The Salford Mennonite Congregation 1717-1988*. Harleysville, Pa.: Salford Mennonite Church,1988.

Augsburger, David. *Dissident Spirituality: A Spirituality of Self-Surrender, Love of God, and Love of Neighbor*. Grand Rapids, Michigan: Brazos Press, 2006.

Augsburger, Myron. *Walking in the Resurrection*. Scottdale, Pa.: Herald Press, 1976.

Barrett, Lois. "Spirituality and Discernment, or How Do You Know if This Spirituality is Christian?" In *The Dilemma of Anabaptist Piety*, 173-181.

Barry, William A. and William J. Connolly. *The Practice of Spiritual Direction*. San Francisco: Harper Collins, 1982.

Bass, Dorothy C., ed. *Practicing Our Faith: A Way of Life for a Searching People*. San Francisco: Jossey-Bass Publishers, 1997.

Bechtel, Arvilla.Shenk *A Medley of Memories: the Recollections of Arvilla Shenk Bechtel*. Morgantown, Pa.: Masthof Press, 2001.

Beck, Ervin and John D. Roth, eds. *Migrant Muses: Mennonite/s Writing in the U.S.* Goshen, Ind.: Mennonite Historical Society, 1998.

Beechy, Atlee. *Seeking Peace: My Journey*. Nappannee, Ind.: Evangel Press, 2001.

Bender, Courtney. "Place, Process, and Practice: Perspectives on Changes in the Character of Mennonite Spirituality." In *The Dilemma of Anabaptist Piety*, 123-130.

Bender, Harold and Cornelius Krahn, C. Henry Smith, eds. *The Mennonite Encyclopedia*. Scottdale, Pa.: Mennonite Publishing House, 1955-1959.

Beyeler, Jodi H. "Author Urges Anabaptist Witness." *Mennonite Weekly Review,* Oct. 30, 2006, 1-2

Boers, Arthur Paul. *On Earth as in Heaven: Justice Rooted in Spirituality.* Scottdale, Pa.: Herald Press, 1991.

Bonhoeffer, Dietrich. *Life Together: The Classic Exploration of Faith in Community.* San Francisco: Harper San Francisco, 2003.

Brooke, Avery. *Hidden in Plain Sight: The Practice of Christian Meditation.* Nashville, Tenn.: The Upper Room, 1978.

Brubaker, Nancy. "Christian Ed Curriculum." Kairos School of Spiritual Formation. P. O. Box 5022, Lancaster, PA 17606-5022, 2004.

Chittister, Joan. *Heart of Flesh: A Feminist Spirituality for Women and Men.* Grand Rapids, Mich.: Wm. B. Erdmans Publishing Company, 1998.

Classen, Susan. *A Spirituality of Service: Freely Give, Freely Receive.* MCC Occasional Paper 29. Akron, Pa.: Mennonite Central Committee, Jan. 2003.

Clements, Teresa, D. M. J. *Missionary Spirituality: For the Praise of His Glory.* Dublin, Ireland: Carmelite Centre of Spirituality, 1987.

Confession of Faith in a Mennonite Perspective. Scottdale, Pa.: Herald Press, 1995.

Conn, Joann Wolski. "Dancing in the Dark: Women's Spirituality and Ministry." In *Handbook of Spirituality for Ministers.* Ed. Robert Wicks. Mahwah, N.J.: Paulist Press, 1995, 77-95.

———. *Spirituality and Personal Maturity.* New York: Paulist Press, 1989.

———.ed. *Women's Spirituality: Resources for Christian Development.* Eugene, Ore.: Wipf & Stock, 2005.

Crawford, James Stewart. "Ignatian Spirituality and the Reformed Tradition." D.Min. Dissertation, Lancaster Theological Seminary, 2007.

Cronk, Sandra. *Dark Night Journey: Inward Repatterning Toward a Life Centered in God.* Wallingford, Pa.: Pendle Hill Publications, 1991.

———.*Gelassenheit: The Rites of the Redemptive Process in Old Order Amish and Old Order Mennonite Communities.* Ph.D. diss., microform, Univ. of Chicago, 1977, cf. *Mennonite Quarterly Review* 55 (1981): 5-44.

Davis, Kenneth R. *Anabaptism and Asceticism.* Scottdale, Pa.: Herald Press, 1974.

De Bhaldraithe, Eoin. "All Who Take the Sword: The Pope on Violence." *Doctrine and Life* dominicanpublications.com (1980).

Dintaman, Stephen F. "The Spiritual Poverty of the Anabaptist Vision." *Conrad Grebel Review* 10 (1992 Spring): 205-208.

———. "Reading the Reactions to the 'Spiritual Poverty of the Anabaptist Vision.'" *Conrad Grebel Review* (1995 Winter): 2-10.

Dueck, Al. "Anabaptists, Pietism, and the Therapeutic Culture." In *The Dilemma of Anabaptist Piety*, 161-172.

Dyck, C. J. Introductory essay. *Spiritual Life in Anabaptism: Classic Devotional Resources*. Scottdale, Pa.: Herald Press, 1995.

Edwards, Tilden. *Spiritual Friend*. Mahwah, N.J.: Paulist Press, 1980.

Elias, Jacob. E-mail to author. Oct. 24, 2002.

Erb, Peter C. "Contemplation and Action in the Modern World." *Conrad Grebel Review* 9.1 (1991 Winter): 1-15.

———. "Spirituality and Mennonite Life." *The Church as Theological Community*. Ed. Harry Huebner. Winnipeg, MB: CMBC Publications, 1990.

Finger, Tom. Abstract of paper for a conference in 2003 called "How Sacramental were the Original Anabaptists?" www.hillsdale.edu/academics/Soc/ritual.htm

FitzGerald, Constance. "The Desire for God and the Transformative Power of Contemplation." In *Light Burdens, Heavy Blessings: Challenges of Church and Culture in the Post Vatican II Era: Essays in Honor of Margaret Brennan*. Ed. Sheehan et al. Quincy, Ill.: Franciscan Press, 2000.

Foster, Richard. *Celebration of Discipline: The Path to Spiritual Growth*. Twentieth Anniversary ed. San Francisco: Harper, 1998.

Frantz, Nadine Pence. "Theological Reflections on Nineteenth Century forms of Piety: Humility, Yieldedness and Denial." In ed. Longenecker, 131-140.

Frey, Miriam. "At the Crossroads: Spiritual Direction in a Mennonite Context." D.Min. thesis, Regis College and the Toronto School of Theology, 2003.

Friedmann, Robert. "Gelassenheit." The *Mennonite Encyclopedia*.

———. *Mennonite Piety through the Centuries*. Goshen, Ind.: Mennonite Historical Society, 1949.

Groff, Ira Kent. *Active Spirituality: A Guide for Seekers and Ministers*. The Alban Institute, 1993.

———. "Theopractice: A New Look at Spirituality" in *Drawing from the Well: Reflections for Praying, Thinking and Acting with Integrity* 1.1, Oasis Ministries, Dec. 2005.

Groff, Thelma and Marcus Smucker. "Spirituality Concerns: A Tentative Proposal for the School Year 1983-84." Archives, Associated Mennonite Biblical Seminary, Elkhart, Ind.

Gross, Leonard, trans. and ed. *Prayer Book for Earnest Christians.* Scottdale, Pa.: Herald Press, 1997.

Guenther, Margaret. *Holy Listening: The Art of Spiritual Direction.* Boston, Massachusetts: Cowley Publications, 1992.

———. *At Home in the World: A Rule of Life for the Rest of Us.* New York: Seabury Books, 2006.

Gundy, Jeff. "Black Goats, Pig-Headed Fathers, and Growing Souls: Some Reflections on the Figure of Harold Bender." *Mennonite Life* 54.4 (1999): 9-14.

Haas, J. Craig. *Readings from Mennonite Writings: New and Old.* Intercourse, Pa.: Good Books, 1992.

Harder, Lydia. "Discipleship Reexamined: Women in the Hermeneutical Community." *The Church as Theological Community.* Ed. Harry Huebner. Winnipeg, MB: Canadian Mennonite Bible College Publications, 1990.

Hauerwas, Stanley. "Confessions of a Mennonite Camp Follower." *Mennonite Quarterly Review* 74.4 (Oct. 2000): 511-522.

———. Quoted in Laurie L. Oswald. "Denomination Leads Interchurch Talks." *The Mennonite,* Sept. 7, 2004, 24.

Hebblethwaite, Margaret. *Motherhood and God.* London: Geoffrey Chapman, 1984.

Hershey, Mary Jane, "A Study of Dress of the Old Mennonites in Franconia Conference 1700-1955." *Pennsylvania Folklife* 9.3 (1958 Summer): 24-45.

Hershey, Ruth, photographs; Phyllis Pellman Good, text. *A Mennonite Woman's Life.* Intercourse, Pa.: Good Books, 1993.

Holmes, Urban T, III. *A History of Christian Spirituality: An Analytical Introduction.* New York: The Seabury Press, 1980.

Hoober Peiffer, Jane, and John Stahl-Wert. *Welcoming New Christians: A Guide for the Christian Initiation of Adults.* Newton, Kan.: Faith & Life Press, 1995.

Hostetler, Beulah S. "Franconia Mennonite Conference and American Protestant Movements 1840-1940." Ph.D. diss., microform, University of Pennsylvania, 1977.

Houser, Gordon. "Passing the Peas". *The Mennonite,* Oct. 15, 2002, 30.

Houser, Mary Lou. *The Spirituality of Ruth Kraybill Souder: Her 103-Year Legacy 1889-1993.* Unpublished manuscript, 1997.

James-Abra, Karen. "An Introduction to an Ancient Christian Ministry: The Practice of Spiritual Direction." *The Conrad Grebel Review* 9.1 (Winter 1991): 15-22.

Johnson, Ben Campbell. *A Seekers Guide to the Christian Faith.* Nashville, Tenn.: Upper Room Books, 2000.

———. *Speaking of God: Evangelism as Initial Spiritual Guidance.* Louisville, Ky.: Westminster Press, 1991.

Kanagy, Conrad L. *Road Signs for the Journey: A Profile of Mennonite Church USA.* Scottdale, Pa.: Herald Press, 2007.

Kauffman, J. Howard and Leo Driedger. *The Mennonite Mosaic: Identity and Modernization.* Scottdale, Pa.: Herald Press, 1991.

Kavanaugh, Kieran and Otilio Rodriguez. *The Collected Works of Saint John of the Cross.* Washington D.C.: Institute of Carmelite Studies, 1991.

Klassen, Pamela. "What's Bre(a)d in the Bone: The Bodily Heritage of Mennonite Women." *Mennonite Quarterly Review* 68 (1994 April): 229-247.

Klaassen, Walter. "Gelassenheit and Creation." *Conrad Grebel Review* 9.1 (Winter 1991): 23-36.

Koenig, John. *New Testament Hospitality: Partnership with Strangers as Promise and Mission.* Philadelphia: Fortress Press, 1985.

Koontz, Gayle Gerber. "RE: research project." E-mail to author. Oct. 24, 2002.

Koontz, Ted, ed. *Godward: Personal Stories of Grace.* Scottdale, Pa.: Herald Press, 1996.

———. Syllabus from class, "Spirituality and Peacemaking," Elkhart, Ind.: Associated Mennonite Biblical Seminary.

———. "RE: research project." E-mail to author. Jan. 23, 2003.

Kraybill, J. Nelson. "The Center of Our Hope." *AMBS Window.* Summer 2003.

Kreider, Alan and Murray, Stuart, eds. *Coming Home: Stories of Anabaptists in Britain and Ireland.* Kitchener, Ont.: Pandora Press, 2000.

Kropf, Marlene and Phyllis Carter. "Contemporary Forms of Spirituality." In *The Dilemma of Anabaptist Piety*, 145-148.

Kropf, Marlene and Eddy Hall. *Praying with the Anabaptists: The Secret of Bearing Fruit.* Newton, Kan.: Faith & Life Press, 1984.

Kropf, Marlene. "Contemplative Spirituality and Contemporary Anabaptist Women." Paper for the series "Catholics and Anabaptists in Conversation about Spirituality." Elizabethtown College, Dec. 3-4, 1997.

———.Personal interview. May 2, 2002. Found in Appendix, Nelson thesis, 2004.

———. "Sisters and Brothers to Keep Us Faithful on the Way." *Gospel Herald,* April 29, 1997.

———. "Female Spirituality." Lecture to class on Spiritual Formation. Lancaster, Pa.: February 2002 (available from author).

Kropf, Marlene and Ken Nafziger. *Singing: A Mennonite Voice.* Scottdale, Pa.: Herald Press, 2001.

Liechty, Daniel, trans. and ed. Introductory essay. *Early Anabaptist Spirituality: Selected Writings.* New York: Paulist Press, 1994.

Liechty, Joseph C. "Humility: The Foundation of Mennonite Religious Outlook in the 1860s." *Mennonite Quarterly Review* 54.1 (1980 Jan.): 5-31.

———. "Mennonites and Conflict in Northern Ireland, 1970-1998." In *From the Ground Up: Mennonite Contributions to International Peacebuilding.* Ed. John Paul Lederach and Cynthia Sampson. Oxford, Eng.: Oxford University Press, 2000.

Linn, Dennis, Sheila Fabricant Linn, and Matthew Linn. *Sleeping with Bread: Holding What Gives You Life.* Mahwah, N.J.: Paulist Press, 1995.

Longacre, Doris Janzen. *More-with-Less Cookbook.* Scottdale, Pa.: Herald Press, 1976.

Longenecker, Stephen, ed. *The Dilemma of Anabaptist Piety.* Bridgewater, Va.: Penobscot Press, 1997.

Maas, Robin and Gabriel O'Donnell. *Spiritual Traditions for the Contemporary Church.* Nashville, Tenn.: Abingdon Press, 1990.

MacIntyre, Alisdair. *After Virtue: A Study in Moral Theology.* 2nd. ed. Notre Dame, Ind.: University of Notre Dame Press, 1984.

MacKinnon, Mary Heather; Moni McIntyre, Mary Ellen Sheehan, eds. *Light Burdens, Heavy Blessings: Challenges of Church and Culture in the Post Vatican II Era: Essays in Honor of Margaret Brennan.* Quincy, Ill. Franciscan Press, May 2000.

Maloney, George A., S.J. *Prayer of the Heart.* Notre Dame, Ind.: Ave Maria Press, 1981.

Martin, Dennis. "Catholic Spirituality and Anabaptist and Mennonite Discipleship." *Mennonite Quarterly Review* 62.1 (Jan.1988): 5-25.

———. "Spiritual Life or Spirituality." *Mennonite Encyclopedia* vol. 5. Ed. Cornelius Dyck and Dennis Martin. Scottdale, Pa.: Herald Press, 1990. Article also available Global Anabaptist Mennonite Encyclopedia Online, www.gameo.org

Martin, John R. *Ventures in Discipleship*. Scottdale, Pa.: Herald Press, 1984.

Mennonite Confession of Faith. Trans. Irvin B. Horst. Adopted April 21, 1632, at Dordrecht, The Netherlands. Lancaster, Pa.: Lancaster Historical Society, 1988.

Miller, Marlin. "A Genuine Biblical Spirituality." *Gospel Herald*, Aug. 31, 1982.

Miller, Wendy. *Learning to Listen: A Guide for Spiritual Friends*. Nashville, Tenn.: Upper Room Books, 1993.

———. *Invitation to Presence: A Guide to Spiritual Disciplines*. Nashville, Tenn.: Upper Room Books, 1995.

Musselman, Julie. "From Anna Baptist and Menno Barbie to Anna Beautiful." *Conrad Grebel Review* (Fall 1998): 92-109.

Muto, Susan. *John of the Cross for Today: The Dark Night*. Notre Dame, Ind.: Ave Maria Press, 1994.

Nelson, Dawn Ruth. "Finding God on Broad Street." Sermon, 1994.

———. "How Do We Become Like Christ? American Mennonite Spiritual Formation Through the Lens of One Woman's Life and One Seminary, 1909-2003." D.Min. thesis, Lancaster Theological Seminary, 2004. The thesis is available from University Microfilms on-line at Proquest.com.

———. "Mennonites and Cistercians in Ireland." *Gospel Herald*, Dec. 9, 1980, 996-997.

———. "Ireland Update." *WMSC VOICE*, Nov. 1984, 4-5.

Nelson, Sarah Ruth. Unpublished manuscript. Goshen College, 2000.

Nouwen, Henri. *Reaching Out: The Three Movements of the Spiritual Life*. Garden City, New York: Doubleday Company, Inc., 1975.

———. "Solitude: The Inner Fabric of Christian Community." *Sojourners*, March 1979.

"A Pastoral Letter on Spirituality from the Ministry of Spirituality Committee." *Gospel Herald*, May 5, 1987, 306-308.

Rempel, John. "Spirituality in Recent Mennonite Writing." *Mennonite Quarterly Review* 71 (Oct. 1997): 595-602.

Roth, John D. *Beliefs: Mennonite Faith and Practice*. Scottdale, Pa.: Herald Press, 2005.

———. "Pietism and the Anabaptist Soul." In *The Dilemma of Anabaptist Piety*, 17-33.

Ruth, Jay. *Looking at Lower Salford*. Souderton, Pa.: Indian Valley Printing Company, 1984.

Ruth, John L. "Re: mission." E-mail to the author, May 24, 2003.

——. *Forgiveness: A Legacy of the West Nickel Mines Amish School.* Scottdale, Pa.: Herald Press, 2007.

——. *Maintaining the Right Fellowship: A Narrative Account of Life in the Oldest Mennonite Community in North America.* Scottdale, Pa.: Herald Press, 1984.

——. *The Earth is the Lord's: A Narrative History of the Lancaster Mennonite Conference.* Scottdale, Pa.: Herald Press, 2001.

Ruth, Susan. Personal interviews. Oct. 2001-Oct. 2002.

——. Unpublished notebooks and diaries of her writing.

Schertz, Mary, ed. "Spirituality," *Vision: A Journal for Church and Theology* 1.1 (2000 Fall).

Schlabach, Theron F. "Mennonites and Pietism in America, 1740-1880: Some Thoughts on the Friedmann Thesis." *Mennonite Quarterly Review* 57 (1983): 222-40.

Schmidt, Kimberly; Diane Zimmerman Umble and Steve Reschly, eds. *Strangers at Home: Amish and Mennonite Women in History.* Baltimore, Md.: The Johns Hopkins University Press , 2002.

Schneiders, Sandra M. I.H.M. *New Wineskins: Re-Imagining Religious life Today.* New York/Mahwah: Paulist Press, 1986.

——*Religious Life in a New Millenium (Volume One) Finding the Treasure: Locating Catholic Religious Life in a New Ecclesial and Cultural Context.* New York/Mahwah, N.J.: Paulist Press, 2000.

Schrag, Jim. "A Study of Mennonites." *Equipping: A Resource Packet for Equipping Mennonite Church USA Pastors and Leaders.* Newton, Kan.: MC USA Communications Offices, Jan. 2007.

Schrag, Paul. "Virtue for the Real World." *Mennonite Weekly Review,* Oct. 23, 2006, 4.

Shenk, Sara Wenger. "Formation Beyond Education: An Interview with Sara Wenger Shenk." *Leader* 4.4 (Summer 2007).

Shisler, Barbara. "Re: update on project." E-mail to the author. March 3, 2002.

Sider, Ron. *The Scandal of the Evangelical Conscience: Why Are Christians Living Just Like the Rest of the World?* Grand Rapids, Mich.: Baker Books, 2005.

Siebert, Bradley. "Forgiveness from the Fringe" *Mennonite Weekly Review,* Oct. 23, 2006, 5.

Smucker, Marcus. "Mennonite Spirituality." *AMBS Bulletin* 50.2 (Winter 1986): 1-3.

——. Personal interview. Jan. 13, 2002. Appendix A, Nelson thesis.

———. "Prayer (Mennonites)." *Mennonite Encyclopedia*, vol. 5; *Global Anabaptist Mennonite Encyclopedia Online*, 1989. Retrieved 4 September 2007, www.gameo.org/encyclopedia/contents/p7365me.html

———. "A Proposal for Spiritual Disciplines at the Associated Mennonite Biblical Seminaries." Elkhart, Ind.: Archives, AMBS. Also printed in Nelson thesis.

———. "A Rationale for Spiritual Guidance in the Mennonite Church." Unpublished essay, 2002.

———. "Self-Sacrifice and Self-Realization in Mennonite Spirituality." Ph.D.diss. The Union Institute and University, 1987.

———. "Spiritual Direction in Mennonite Perspective." *Mennonite Encyclopedia*, vol. 5.

Snyder, Arnold, ed. *Biblical Concordance of the Swiss Brethren, 1540.* Scottdale, Pa.: Pandora Press, 2001.

———. "Issues in Spirituality." *Conrad Grebel Review* 9.1 (Winter 1991): v-vii.

———. "Modern Mennonite Reality and Anabaptist Spirituality: Balthasar Hubmaier's Catechism of 1526." *Conrad Grebel Review* 9.1 (Winter 1991): 37-53.

———. "The Monastic Origins of Swiss Anabaptist Sectarianism." *Mennonite Quarterly Review* 57 (1983): 5-26.

Stoltzfus, Louise. *Amish Women: Lives and Stories.* Intercourse, Pa.: Good Books, 1994.

———. *Quiet Shouts: Stories of Lancaster Mennonite Women Leaders.* Scottdale, Pa.: Herald Press, 1999.

Stutzman, Rose Mary, ed. *Soul Care: How to Plan and Guide Inspirational Retreats.* Scottdale, Pa.: Herald Press, 2003.

Syllabi from the AMBS spiritual formation program since 1983, copied in Appendix D, Nelson thesis.

Thayer, Anne. E-mail to author. Feb. 12, 2003.

Van Braght, Tieleman Jansz. *The Martyr's Mirror.* Scottdale, Pa.: Herald Press, 1950.

Veltri, John, SJ. *Week of Directed Prayer in a Church Setting: A Manual.* Available from Office of Religious Education, Diocese of Hamilton, 700 King Street West, Hamilton, Ontario L8P 1C7.

Waltner, Erland. E-mails to author. Jan. 18-20, 2003.

Wiens, Delbert. "From the Village to the City: A Grammar for the Languages We Are," *Direction* (Oct. 1973-Jan. 1974); http://www.directionjournal.org/article?89

Wilson, Jonathan R. *Living Faithfully in a Fragmented World: Lessons for the Church from MacIntyre's After Virtue.* Harrisburg, Pa.: Trinity Press International, 1997.

"Women, Therapy and Spiritual Direction: Seeing with Spiritual Eyes the Psychological Struggles, Experiences and Faith Development of Women." Eastern College Conference notebook, St. Davids, Pa. May 30-June 1, 1996.

Wuthnow, Robert. "The Changing Character of American Spirituality." In *The Dilemma of Anabaptist Piety,* 109-120.

———. *After Heaven: Spirituality in America Since the 1950's.* Berkeley, Calif.: University of California Press, 1998.

Yoder, John Howard. *The Politics of Jesus: Vicit Agnus Noster.* 2nd. ed. Grand Rapids: Eerdmans, 1994.

Recent Recommendations

Boers, Arthur Paul; Barbara Nelson Gingerich, Eleanor Kreider, John D. Rempel and Mary H. Schertz. *Take Our Moments and Our Days: An Anabaptist Prayer Book. Advent through Pentecost.* Elkhart, Ind.: Institute of Mennonite Studies and Scottdale, Pa.: Herald Press, 2007.

Boers, Arthur Paul, Barbara Nelson Gingerich, Eleanor Kreider, John D. Rempel, and Mary H. Schertz. *Take Our Moments and Our Days. Ordinary Time.* Elkhart, Ind.: Institute of Mennonite Studies, 2005.

Kanagy, Conrad L. *Road Signs for the Journey: A Profile of Mennonite Church USA.* Scottdale, Pa.: Herald Press, 2007.

Miller, Wendy J. *Jesus Our Spiritual Director: A Pilgrimage through the Gospels.* Nashville, Tenn.: Upper Room Books, 2004.

Snyder, Arnold C. *Following in the Footsteps of Christ: The Anabaptist Tradition.* Ed. Philip Sheldrake. Traditions of Christian Spirituality Series. Maryknoll, N.Y.: Orbis Books, 2004.

THE AUTHOR

Dawn Ruth Nelson, Harleysville, Pennsylvania, is a Mennonite pastor and spiritual director. Born in Sellersville, Pennsylvania, she grew up in suburbs of Philadelphia and Boston almost in but definitely not of a Mennonite subculture in the 1950s and 1960s—her family was Mennonite but her friends and neighbors were not—and her early dream was to be a folksinger in the mold of Dave van Ronk and Buffy St. Marie.

The sense of being in two worlds, of being marginal, has led her to do work on the margins of the Mennonite world—she was part of the first Mennonite peace witness in Ireland from 1979-1991 and then worked as chaplain with people with disabilities for ten years, trying to bring marginalized people more into the center of the church.

Currently she serves as the first woman pastor of a small diverse Mennonite congregation on the fringe of Franconia Mennonite Conference. She has studied in United Church of Christ and Mennonite seminaries and at Neumann (Catholic) College.

Nelson's sense of call to ministry developed before there were many women ministers in the Mennonite church. Her first description of what she wanted to do in ministry was to be a "soul nurse." Since then seminary, spiritual direction training, and motherhood have also prepared her for the task that is pastoring. Her husband Paul is a valued co-worker, and watching her children—Sarah, Pete and Ben—turn into adults brings her much joy. She enjoys reading, writing, e-mailing, birds, chocolate, lots of movies, playing piano and guitar, walking, and silence. She is a board member and grateful participant in the Kairos School of Spiritual Formation.